D1402716

Wild and Young

Wild
and Young

Editor: Ann Lloyd

Consultant Editor: David Robinson

Orbis Publishing·London

© Orbis Publishing Limited, London 1983

First published in the United Kingdom by
Orbis Publishing Limited, London

This edition marketed in the United States
of America by RCA Direct Marketing Inc.,
1133 Avenue of the Americas, New York,
New York 10036, U.S.A.

All rights reserved. No part
of this publication may be reproduced,
stored in a retrieval system, or transmitted
in any form or by any means, electronic, mechanical,
photocopying, recording or otherwise, without prior
permission of the publishers

Printed and bound in Spain by
Graficromo, S.A. Cordoba

Frontispiece: Troy Donahue and Sandra Dee in
A Summer Place (1959)

Contents

Abbreviations used in text

add: additional; **adv:** advertising; **anim:** animation;
art dir: art direction; **ass:** assistant; **assoc:** associate; **chor:** choreography;
col: colour process; **comm:** commentary; **cont:** continuity; **co-ord:** co-ordination;
cost: costume; **dec:** decoration; **des:** design; **dial:** dialogue; **dial dir:** dialogue direction;
dir: direction; **doc:** documentary; **ed:** film editing; **eng:** engineer; **ep:** episode;
exec: executive; **loc:** location; **lyr:** lyrics; **man:** management; **mus:** music; **narr:** narration;
photo: photography; **prod:** production; **prod co:** production company; **prod sup:** production
supervision; **rec:** recording; **rel:** released: **r/t:** running time; **sc:** scenario/screenplay/script;
sd: sound; **sp eff:** special effects; **sup:** supervision; **sync:** synchronization;
sys: system. Standard abbreviations for countries are used. Most are
self-evident but note: A = Austria; AUS = Australia; GER = Germany
and West Germany after 1945; E.GER = East Germany.

No-one would expect to find a Mary Pickford picture included in the category of horror films. Yet *Sparrows* is not only one of Pickford's finest movies, it also has an honoured place in William K. Everson's book on the horror genre.

Perhaps its inclusion there is not quite fair. The villain, Grimes, superbly played by that great character actor Gustav von Seyffertitz, is certainly a horrifying creation, and though there is one scene which for sheer, sustained tension has seldom been equalled, the overall atmosphere is rather different. *Sparrows* is a melodrama – a cruel, frightening Dickensian melodrama – played perfectly straight and with utter conviction. It is also a film virtually without a hero. With Pickford as its heroine, and a villain like von Seyffertitz, it simply has no need of one.

The Southern swamp in which the film is set was constructed on the back-lot of the Mary Pickford Company studio on Santa Monica Boulevard, and no location shooting could equal the impact of this magnificent design by art director Harry Oliver, one of the great forgotten artists of the Twenties. This swamp has quicksands, a mass of hostile greenery and a lavish supply of alligators, and provides the nastiest of settings for the supremely nasty Mr Grimes, a baby-farmer of repellent mien and utter savagery.

The scene in which Mary Pickford as Mama Mollie – the girl who plays mother, nurse and comforter to the smaller inmates of Grimes' farm – leads them to safety across the swamp, has set historians at loggerheads. The climax of the journey sees Mollie walking along a log across a corner of the swamp, carrying one baby on her back with the others following, and alligators snapping their jaws within a couple of feet of the convoy. The story has it that Douglas Fairbanks visited the set, saw his wife in danger, was enraged and said that double-exposures should have been used. Miss Pickford herself told this to interviewers, and it was generally accepted.

The film historian Booton Henderson, however, interviewed Hal Mohr – one of three notable cameramen who worked on *Sparrows* – who gave a very different account. According to Mohr, the alligators were filmed first, with the top half of the picture matted out; Miss Pickford and the children did their bit two days later. Mohr adds a lovely detail. Out of camera range a trainer threw meat to the alligators; Mohr carefully timed the opening jaws; and two days later Mary could stumble at exactly the points of greatest danger. The more alarming version must have been circulated as studio publicity, and time and nostalgia have provided the rest.

Mary Pickford's own performance is of the kind she did superbly well, falling as it does mid-way between her little-girl roles and her adults. She was 32 at the time, playing a character of about 17, and

Sparrows

she looks precisely right. It was the last occasion she would play a child, and her sturdy, spirited Mollie was a marvellous end to that side of her career.

There are other notable performances. William Beaudine, a skilful director of children, coaxes Mary's bedraggled brood into the most woebegone naturalism. Young Spec O'Donnell – splendid as the little Jewish kid in *Little Annie Rooney* (1925) – offers a very different characterization as Grimes' callous son, Ambrose. And the half-witted Mrs Grimes is nicely managed by Charlotte Mineau.

Perhaps the film's greatest virtues are those which were taken for granted in the Twenties, and rarely noticed in the criticism of the time, remarkable though they may appear today. *Sparrows* has not dated. It survives, and survives proudly, by virtue of its enormous care for detail, the perfection of its camerawork, and a total belief in what was being done, sufficient to inspire everyone involved.

Sometimes it seems as though the Twenties did not deserve their movies. Mordaunt Hall, film critic for the *New York Times*, had little use for *Sparrows*, and dismissed its 'puerile ideas' and 'exaggerated suspense'. Fortunately, the public generally knew better.

JACK LODGE

Directed by William Beaudine, 1926
Prod co: United Artists. **sc:** Winifred Dunn, George Marion Jr, C. Gardner Sullivan. **photo:** Charles Rosher, Hal Mohr, Karl Struss. **ed:** Harold McLernon. **art dir:** Harry Oliver. **ass dir:** Tom McNamara, Carl Harbough, Earle Brown. **length:** 7763 feet (approx. 103 minutes); recent soundtrack version 81 minutes.
Cast: Mary Pickford (*Mollie*), Roy Stewart (*Dennis Wayne*), Mary Louise Miller (*Doris Wayne*), Gustav von Seyffertitz (*Mr Grimes*), Charlotte Mineau (*Mrs Grimes*), Spec O'Donnell (*Ambrose*), Lloyd Whitlock (*Bailey*).

After the triumph of *Shoulder Arms* (1918) Chaplin made *Sunnyside* (1919), which was a comparative failure. In 1919, with his marriage to Mildred Harris already showing signs of strain, he was at a crisis of self-doubt. He relates in his autobiography that he would go to his studio, day after day, along with his stock company of actors in the hope of inspiration that never came.

Just when he had despaired of finding a new idea, he went to the Orpheum music hall where Jack Coogan was appearing in his eccentric dancing act. Coogan's four-year-old son Jackie made a brief appearance along with him, and Chaplin was so engaged by the little boy's personality and way with an audience that he promptly began thinking up a scenario that would team the child and the Tramp. Jack Coogan had just signed a short-term contract with Fatty Arbuckle but the child was still free and Chaplin quickly hired him; as he recalls in his autobiography, the father's words were: 'Why, of course you can have the little punk.'

Jackie Coogan played Charlie's younger son in *A Day's Pleasure* (1919) as a preliminary to his major role in *The Kid*. Chaplin found the child a natural performer and quick learner:

'There were a few basic rules to learn in pantomime and Jackie very soon mastered them. He could apply emotion to the action and action to the emotion, and could repeat it time and again without losing the effect of spontaneity.'

The very real affection that grew up between Chaplin and Jackie is quite evident in *The Kid*. According to Chaplin, the poignant scene where Jackie cries real tears as the orphanage men are taking him away was achieved by the simple ruse of Jackie's father threatening that if he did not cry, he would be taken away from the studio to the real workhouse.

The film opened with a title: 'A picture with a smile – perhaps a tear.' Although previous Chaplin films had introduced sentiment and pathos, this was the first time in the history of film comedy that anyone had risked mingling a highly dramatic, near-tragic story with comedy and farce.

The film was also much longer – six reels, or 88 minutes at silent running speed – than any he had previously made. With his customary care (the one-minute scene of Charlie and Jackie's pancake breakfast is said to have taken two weeks and 50,000 feet of negative to achieve), his shooting schedule was long and costly. The sum of nearly $500,000 which he claimed to have invested was enormous for a comedy at that date.

It was completed under extreme difficulties. Mildred Harris was in the process of divorcing him by the time he was editing. Fearing that her lawyers might attempt to seize the film, Chaplin smuggled 500 reels of film to Salt Lake City, where the picture was cut in a hotel room, with only a small, elementary cutting machine on which to view the

This is the great picture upon which the famous comedian has worked a whole year.

6 reels of Joy.

Charles Chaplin IN **"THE KID"**

Written and directed by Charles Chaplin

A First National ⦾ Attraction

Directed by Charles Chaplin, 1921
Prod co: Charles Chaplin Productions, for First National. **prod:** Charles Chaplin. **assoc dir:** Charles (Chuck) Reisner. **sc:** Charles Chaplin. **photo:** Roland H. (Rollie) Totheroh. **length:** 5300 feet (approx. 88 minutes).
Cast: Charles Chaplin (*Tramp*), Edna Purviance (*mother*), Jackie Coogan (*boy*), Carl Miller (*artist-author*), Tom Wilson (*policeman*), Henry Bergman (*superintendent of the night shelter*), Chuck Reisner (*tough*), Lita Grey (*a flirtatious angel*), Phyllis Allen (*woman with the pram*), Nelly Bly Baker (*slum nurse*), Albert Austin (*man staying overnight in the shelter*), Jack Coogan (*pickpocket*).

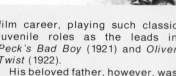

material. Even when a preview was arranged at the local movie theatre, Chaplin had still not seen the finished picture on a screen. His inevitable apprehensions proved unfounded; from this very first screening, audiences responded wholeheartedly to the film, accepting totally the mixture of moods from high sentiment to low comedy.

Critics were not all so convinced. The playwright J. M. Barrie was among those who found the dream sequence out of place, which perhaps it is, though it is delightful with its slum angels (one of whom was, by chance, Chaplin's future wife, Lita Grey). Others were rather stuffy about 'vulgarities' such as Charlie's investigation of the foundling's sex, a joke about the child's dampness and the con-

sequent devising of toilet facilities. Today such endearingly truthful touches have ceased to shock. The sentimental elements are more alien to modern audiences; and when, almost half a century later, Chaplin reissued the film with new music of his own composition, he trimmed some shots that he felt would be unacceptable to a new public. He need hardly have worried. The film, his comic invention and Jackie Coogan's remarkable performance have lost none of their power – it is one of the most durable of all silent movies.

The Kid made Jackie Coogan a star and world-wide celebrity. His trip to Europe, when he was received by the Pope, monarchs and presidents, was a royal progress. He went on to a highly profitable

film career, playing such classic juvenile roles as the leads in *Peck's Bad Boy* (1921) and *Oliver Twist* (1922).

His beloved father, however, was killed in a road accident; and when, with adolescence and manhood, he found his star waning, his mother and stepfather withheld from him what was left of his earnings. Most of what remained was lost in lawsuits. This case had permanent results in the Californian legislation known as 'The Coogan Act' to secure half of the earnings of minors for their own future use. In later years Coogan, with no trace left of his cute baby looks, made occasional film appearances; and on television played the grotesque Uncle Fester in *The Addams Family*.   DAVID ROBINSON

2

3

6

5

7

8

An unmarried mother (1) leaves her baby in an empty wedding limousine with a note asking the finder to care for the child. The car is stolen, and the thieves dump the baby in the slums where he is discovered by Charlie, a Tramp (2). Charlie's efforts to get rid of the child are all frustrated (3), and he is obliged to take him into his own garret room where he ingeniously devises a cradle, feeding bottles and other necessities.

Five years later (4) Charlie is a glazier; the boy precedes him around the street breaking windows. After a doctor has examined him (5), the child-care authorities try to take the little boy off to an orphanage; but Charlie manages to rescue him from the truck that is carrying him away. Now fugitives (6), they pass the night in a doss-house among outcasts and thieves.

Meanwhile the mother, who has become a rich and famous singer, has by chance discovered the whereabouts of her long-lost and sought-after child. Learning of the reward she is offering, the superintendent of the doss-house snatches the child while Charlie is sleeping and takes him off (7) to the police station.

Later Charlie, exhausted from seeking the child, dreams that the slums have been transformed into a paradise inhabited by angels and kindliness (8). He is awakened by a policeman – the mother has sent for Charlie to reunite him with the boy.

Tol'able David

1

The film rights of the novelist Joseph Hergesheimer's short story, *Tol'able David*, were purchased by D.W. Griffith, who planned to film it with the star Richard Barthelmess. When Barthelmess left Griffith in 1920, he bought the property from Griffith and took it with him to the newly-formed company, Inspiration Pictures. Henry King was assigned to direct.

It was a providential sequence of events. Seldom have director, star and story been so perfectly in harmony. The story is set in Virginia, where King was born, and takes place around the time of the director's own childhood in the 1890s. Charles Duell, the head of Inspiration Pictures, wanted the film to be made in Pennsylvania, but King insisted that it be shot on Virginian locations – 'the pastoral valley of Greenstream', where the action takes place, was in fact the village of Crabbottom, and the surrounding countryside, not far from King's birthplace.

King's best films have been celebrations of the small towns, the villages and the open spaces of America. This feature, enhanced by Henry Cronjager's radiant photography, is aptly conveyed in *Tol'able David*. King's intense understanding of, and sympathy with, the manners and tempo of a life which he had himself known, give the film a deep conviction.

Tol'able David is said to have been an important influence on the Russian film-makers Sergei Eisenstein and V. I. Pudovkin. If it was, it cannot have been through any bravura passages of direction or striking editing, for King's style here is one of total simplicity. The Russians had learnt the basic grammar of film-making from Griffith's work; but from King they could appreciate the significance of movement within the frame and the function of the camera as a quiet observer rather than as an eager participant imposing itself on the dramatic situation.

Until the shadows fall half way through the film, with David's brother crippled and his father dead, there is no more than a hint of disturbance of the pastoral dream in *Tol'able David*; and King is content to watch his characters live their parts, viewing them with humour, with admiration, and occasionally, with a tiny touch of irony.

The film's richness of detail is one of its lasting strengths. David playing his harmonica as he drives his cows down the lane, leading in to the little knife-throwing game of mumplety-peg with Esther, and foreshadowing his dance of sheer happiness in the moonlight later, where again the harmonica appears; old Kinemon, introduced by an intertitle presenting him as a pillar of Old Testament virtues, and first seen, immediately after, yawning happily over his comic book; the delicious comedy centring on the dog Rocket, forever embarrassing David's courtship, yet doing it with such charm that his death comes as an almost unbearable surprise – all these sketches of daily life and much more help King to create an ambiance of complete naturalism, so that the audience remains as convinced when the melodrama of the second half comes along.

Richard Barthelmess at 25 was a little old for the part of David, but he contrived to look much younger, and his characteristic blending of vulnerability and interior resource is exactly right. There are pleasures, too, in the performances of others much less familiar – Gladys Hulette's Esther is a delightfully unaffected heroine; Forrest Robinson as her grandfather, caught between his lethal cousins and his friends, conveys perfectly a good and simple man overwhelmed by events; and perhaps best of all, Patterson Dial as David's sister-in-law Rose, quiet and still in her grief, catches perfectly the timelessness and universality of King's vision.

The only flaw in the film, and it is a small one, is the exaggeration of Ernest Torrence's mannerisms as the most evil of the Hatburns. But as film historian William K. Everson wrote, 'dear old Ernest, with that same slobbering and hogging, livened up many a dull picture on other occasions, and he really had no way of knowing (especially so early in his career) that this time he was appearing in a classic.'

Finally, mention should be made of the excellence of the intertitles throughout the film. *Tol'able David* carries no credit for titling, but as King did largely remodel the script, he may well have had some hand in the titles as well. They are taut and pointed, they make no effort to provide dialogue which the audience does better to imagine, and they unfailingly summon up a mood to reinforce that of the images. Good titling adds enormously to the strength of a silent film, and may contribute greatly to the making of a genuine masterpiece like *Tol'able David*.   JACK LODGE

David Kinemon lives on a farm in Virginia with his parents, his elder brother Allen, whom he admires, and Allen's wife Rose (1). Life in the village is gentle; the great event of the day is the

---

Directed by Henry King, 1921
Prod co: Inspiration Pictures, for First National. **prod:** Henry King. **sc:** Edmund Goulding, Henry King, based on the short story by Joseph Hergesheimer. **photo:** Henry Cronjager. **ed:** Duncan Mansfield. **length:** 7118 ft (35mm) (118 minutes).
Cast: Richard Barthelmess (*David Kinemon*), Gladys Hulette (*Esther Hatburn*), Walter P. Lewis (*Iscah Hatburn*), Ernest Torrence (*Luke Hatburn*), Ralph Yearsley (*Luke's brother*), Forrest Robinson (*Grandpa Hatburn*), Edmund Gurney (*David's father*), Marion Abbott (*David's mother*), Warner Richmond (*Allen*), Patterson Dial (*Rose*), Laurence Eddinger (*Mr Galt*), Henry Hallam (*doctor*).

3

5

7

arrival of the passenger and mail hack, regularly driven by Allen. David dreams of the day when he will drive the hack (2), but his parents tell him that he is not yet a real man, 'just tol'able'. Meanwhile, he is falling in love with Esther (3), grand-daughter of Mr Hatburn, a neighbour.

Three Hatburn cousins, fugitives from the law, take refuge in the Hatburn house. One of them, Luke, a psychopath who delights in cruelty, wantonly kills David's dog (4); when Allen intervenes, Luke fells him with a rock and tramples on him (5). Allen is permanently paralysed, and his father dies of a heart attack while attempting to avenge him. David is persuaded by his

mother not to risk his own life by confronting the Hatburns (6).

David and Esther become estranged for a while, and David begins to feel that he is regarded as a coward. He later finds work in the local store when the Kinemons are forced to leave their farm. Then one day, when the driver is drunk, David gets his chance to drive the hack.

Luke Hatburn maliciously steals the mail, and also threatens Esther, who escapes him. In the course of a savage fight, David wounds or kills the villainous Hatburn cousins (7). Esther has alerted the villagers but, before they can act, David, battered and bloody, brings the mail in (8). At last, he is considered a man.

8

Babes in Hollywood

The juvenile giants who took Hollywood by storm

From the moment in 1895 when, in front of Monsieur Lumière's cine camera, a grinning boy put his foot on the gardener's hose-pipe, and then when the mystified old man peered into the nozzle took his foot off again, children became an irresistible force in the movies. Early films abound in mischievous boys and angelic little girls – or occasionally vice versa. Even babies were popular screen heroes.

It was only in 1911 that film actors began to be credited by name, but many professional children – such as Mary Pickford's kid brother Jack, Adèle de Garde, Yale Boss, Gladys Egan, John Tansey and Paul Kelly – were already familiar faces to cinemagoers. One of the child stars, a particularly effete curly-head called Kenneth Casey, actually composed and published a song in his own honour:

> Just because I am the Moving Picture Boy,
> That is why I'm everybody's love and joy.
> Every time my face is flashed upon the screen
> They say: Oh, he's the sweetest thing we've ever seen . . .

Within the next few years the cult of personality mushroomed, and kids like Bobby Connelly, Helen Badgley, Andy Clark and Marie Osborne starred in their own one- or two-reeler series, dishing out the comedy and, when needed, the pathos. But the first child stars of feature-length films emerged at the beginning of the Twenties: 13-year-old Wesley Barry in *Dinty* (1920) and Jackie Coogan (seven years his junior) in Chaplin's *The Kid* (1921). Supremacy in short kid films – almost totally reserved for broad comedy from now on – was wrapped up for good the following year when Hal Roach launched the Our Gang series, an institution that was to last till 1944, with endless imitators but no equals.

Wesley Barry and his successor Ben Alexander only enjoyed two or three years of child stardom. Jackie Coogan, having got to the top that much younger, stayed there for a whole decade, right into the early years of talkies. It i[s] forgotten now what a superstar Coogan was. He was 'merchandized' in the same way th[e] Beatles and Snoopy have been in our time[:] there were Coogan caps, Coogan dolls, Cooga[n] match-holders, the lot. In 1924, not yet ten, h[e] toured America and Europe in aid of a[n] orphans' fund, in the course of which he wa[s] received by the League of Nations in Genev[a] and in Rome by the Pope, who bestowed o[n] him the Gold Cross of the Order of Jerusalem[.] Making only two or three films a year, he ha[d] earned a small fortune by 1925. As late[r] transpired, he might just as well have saved hi[s] time – and in fact did so for the last three year[s] of the Twenties as far as films were concerned[:] he was mainly occupied in an interminabl[e] vaudeville tour of the world with his father.

Coogan bluffed

The talkies tempted Jackie Coogan back to th[e] studios. Now 15, he starred in *Tom Sawye[r]* (1930), and as Tom again in *Huckleberry Fin[n]* (1931). Here his childhood ended, in ever[y] sense. He was too old to continue in boy part[s] and in 1935 his much-loved father died in a ca[r] crash (taking with him in the tangle of meta[l] Jackie's ex-Huck, Junior Durkin).

Mrs Coogan then married the family's finan[-] cial adviser and they proceeded to spend mos[t] of the money her son had earned over th[e] previous decade or so. Jackie asked for it to b[e] paid over to him, but they said there had neve[r] been any question of the money being hi[s.] When a year or two later he married Bett[y] Grable (still relatively unknown) he was ob[-] liged to go to law in an attempt to get hi[s] mother and stepfather to pay up; but what h[e] finally secured barely covered the legal fees [of] the lengthy case. The scandal did, howeve[r]

Above: Jackie Coogan rose to stardom as the waif adopted by Charles Chaplin in The Kid. *He did not, however, get to see the film for several years: 'Chaplin previewed it the first time about 9 o'clock at night – and that was past my bedtime.' Right: Hal Roach's 1933 version of Our Gang in the comedy short* The Kid From Borneo *(1933). From left, Spanky McFarland, Stymie Beard, Dickie Moore, Dorothy De Borba, Tommy Bond, Pete the Pup*

ad to the passing of a law – now updated, but still generally known as the Coogan Law – which obliges parents or guardians to keep half of child actors' earnings in trust for their adulthood.

Jackie Coogan at any rate, if nearly over the hill, was automatically Prince of the Child Stars when the Thirties opened; but there were others who successfully negotiated the switch to sound. Leon Janney (b.1917) for instance – a cheerful, curly blond who had acted earlier under the name of Leon Ramon – was a veteran of some 50 film appearances, including some with Our Gang in 1927. He scored a big hit in 1930 as the loyal child in *Courage*, and had several leading boy parts over the next two years, after which he followed Coogan into the mists of adolescence.

Jackie Cooper, superstar

A bigger star than Leon Janney – also a former member of Our Gang, and a leading one from 1929 – was to hit the jackpot in 1931. Jackie Cooper (b.1922) had been in films from the age of three. In 1931 his uncle, who happened to be the director Norman Taurog and had got him before the cameras in the first place, gave him the lead in a kid film called *Skippy*, based on a popular comic strip. The film was a corker. Cooper, already well known from Our Gang, became a major star and won an Oscar nomination for his performance – as he was to do again later in the year when teamed with Wallace Beery in *The Champ* (1931). Another three Jackie Cooper films – including a sequel to *Skippy* – were squeezed into 1931, and over the next four years he starred in ten more, three of them, like *Treasure Island* (1934), reuniting him with Beery.

Cooper was not a handsome boy: a somewhat baleful and peevish little face, thatched with stringy blond hair, centred on a strangely pursy mouth with a lower lip which at times of defiance or misery stuck out like a rainspout. He was a lachrymose tough, a formidable weeper. This doesn't take into account, however, his immense spontaneity (at least to begin with), his humour and temperament. He was able to exist, or seem to, quite unselfconsciously in front of the camera, with a relaxed insouciance which was charming; but when

Above: Leon Janney in Courage. *His movie career faded when he grew too old for child parts, but he has since become a well-known actor on TV, stage and radio. Centre: Baby Peggy Montgomery, winsome star of the early Twenties. Top left and top: the familiar faces of Jackie Cooper – weeping his way to an Oscar nomination in* Skippy, *and sticking out his lower lip in* The Devil Is a Sissy *(1936), with Mickey Rooney and Freddie Bartholomew*

he had an emotional scene to play, he went at it with impressive, uningratiating passion. By 1934 there began to be murmurs of disenchantment from the public, and some critics mentioned an increase in mannerism. Soon the terrible teens were upon him and in the late Thirties his career gently dimmed. After the war he returned – a far better-looking fellow – and played leads in one or two unremarkable movies and some Broadway plays before ending up in TV as actor and producer. Since 1948 he has made only two or three film appearances.

The mean kid

Cast as Cooper's pet hate in *Skippy*, back in 1931, was a highly interesting and amusing child actor called Jackie Searl (b.1920). Now almost forgotten, he made twice as many films as Cooper did in his childhood, and while he was never a star, his parts were meaty and rewarding. Searl specialized in playing mean, sneaky little runts – arrogant, smirking, prissy, insufferable. He perfected the role of a sort of Machiavellian milksop, and if the good little toughs like Cooper were allowed to rout him in the end, it wasn't before he had inflicted considerable torment on them along the way. At a time when most Hollywood kids were busting their guts to be tough and likeable, it was a shrewd move to be The Kid You Love to Hate, and Jackie Searl did very nicely out of it. He proved an admirable foil, later on, to the tomboy Jane Withers.

Another of the tough-and-likeables, of course, was Mickey Rooney (b.1922), whose real name was Joe Yule Jr, and who was born more or less in the proverbial trunk, of Irish-American vaudeville parents. Impossible to keep off the stage, he joined the family act at the age of two, and by four was a celebrated dancer. Aged six, he made his first screen appearance – as a midget – and soon afterwards won the coveted leading role in a comic strip series: the Mickey McGuire comedies which ran from 1927 to 1932.

These were the most successful of the many two-reeler kid series that attempted to challenge Hal Roach's Our Gang. From now on Joe Yule Jr *was* Mickey McGuire; in the next five years, which took him from silent films into

Above: Freddie Bartholomew. dubbed the 'George Arliss of child actors' by Time *magazine. as David Copperfield. with W.C. Fields as Micawber. Centre: Bartholomew later dropped out of* Thoroughbreds Don't Cry *to be replaced by another young British actor. Ronald Sinclair (on Sophie Tucker's right). but the film's main distinction was the teaming. for the first time. of Mickey Rooney and Judy Garland. Top: Jackie Cooper as Jim Hawkins and Wallace Beery as Silver in* Treasure Island. *Top right: Bartholomew in* Little Lord Fauntleroy *with Dolores Costello as his mother. Above right: Rooney in* Young Tom Edison *(1940)*

talkies. he adopted it as his professional name as well as that of the character he played. He wore short pants and braces. big boots and a shredded bowler hat. He was bossy. bumptious and. some complained. tiresomely precocious in his mannerisms: but no-one could deny his sheer energy or the force of his personality. Oddly enough. both he and (later) Shirley Temple were turned down by Our Gang before making the big time on their own.

Rooney at the top

When Mickey left the McGuire series in 1932. he lost his entitlement to the name too. and as the Yules had split up some years earlier. a new one was needed. He became Mickey Rooney (apparently Looney was considered at one point) and appeared in some 25 films over the next three years. often giving a lift to otherwise feeble entertainments. A major surprise in 1935 was his casting and subsequent triumph as Puck in Max Reinhardt and William Dieterle's film version of *A Midsummer Night's Dream*: though the manic cackle was overdone. his wild capering sprite was a real creation. The little horns looked quite in place and one would not have been surprised to see his knees bend backwards.

In 1936 he was teamed with the genteel Freddie Bartholomew in *Little Lord Fauntleroy*. the tough and toffee-nosed contrast was so piquant that it was repeated thrice in the next three years. In 1937 Rooney made his first appearance as the irrepressible teenager Andy Hardy in *A Family Affair*: this led to a series of over a dozen Andy Hardy films. Also in 1937. in *Thoroughbreds Don't Cry*. he was matched for the first time with 15-year-old Judy Garland. a partnership that was to mature in the better-remembered *Babes in Arms* (1939) and *Strike Up the Band* (1940).

It will not have escaped the notice of mathematicians that Mickey Rooney was by now in his late teens and even less a child actor than

was Garland. Yet he went on playing teenag parts into the Forties. until incipient tubbines drove him into screen adulthood. Over thirt years later he is still full of bounce. and once o twice in a decade turns in a really goo performance.

Tots for the talkies

All of the child stars looked at so far were i action. one way or another. before the arriva of the talkies. One new problem talkies ha brought to Hollywood was that of findin suitable voices for English subjects. particu larly adaptations of English literary classic where the accents of Brooklyn or Los Angele might fracture credibility. Aristocratic-lookin children like Ben Alexander or Philippe D Lacy had been convincing 'little gentlemen' i the Twenties. but those times were past. Dicki Moore. an angelic little chap from Our Gang and one of the busiest child film actors of th Thirties. starred in a 1933 version of *Olive Twist*. but it didn't please many.

Around this time. MGM started planning David Copperfield (1935). British actors lik Frank Lawton. Elizabeth Allan. Basil Rath bone. Maureen O'Sullivan. and Roland Youn were approached. But who would play th child Copperfield? Louis B. Mayer wante Jackie Cooper: but Cooper was not precisel your little Englishman. and so studio scout were sent across the Atlantic. In London the met a determined maiden lady called Millicen Bartholomew. chaperoning her self-possesse nine-year-old nephew. Frederick Llewellyn. H was highly rated. she told them. in amateu circles in Warminster. Wiltshire. and at th Italia Conti Stage School. His parents ha given her permission to promote Freddie career. and he had already had small parts in brace of British films.

Freddie gave the visitors a taste of hi quality. and they made favourable noises: bu Government regulations forbade a child of tha

ge to work abroad, so the scouts returned
mpty-handed to Hollywood, half resigned to
ooper as Young David. Time passed, and the
lm still hadn't been set up. But during that
me Miss Bartholomew had travelled to the
SA with her nephew, quite informally and
oincidentally, 'to visit relatives'. Out of pure
oliteness she and Freddie (he dressed as David
opperfield) dropped in to say hello to the
ce men at MGM: and before you could say
ckie Cooper, Freddie had the part and a
even-year contract.

From 1935 to 1938 Freddie Bartholomew
as a name to conjure with. He played Garbo's
on in *Anna Karenina* (1935), the title role in
ttle Lord Fauntleroy (1936), leads in *Captains*
ourageous (1937) and *Kidnapped* (1938). He
as cast repeatedly opposite his perfect foil, the
xuberantly 'common' Mickey Rooney.
artholomew's screen persona was cool, intel-
gent and haughtily sensitive, but always
issy. Privately, he had troubles. His some-
hat offhand parents, back in England, sud-
enly showed a furious interest in their famous
ild, and accused 'Aunt Cissie' (whom he'd
rown very close to) of something approach-
g kidnap. Hideous and protracted legal
rangles followed, and when they petered out
conclusively Bartholomew, like Coogan
efore him, had lost nearly all he had earned.
nd by the end of the Thirties, his film career,
s a child at least, was over.

ittle French kings
rance, too, had a little Prince of the Screen
uring the Thirties, who found fame before
artholomew did. The frail, skinny Robert
ynen (1922–43) was desperately moving in
lien Duvivier's *Poil de Carotte* (1932, Carrot-
ead) as the unloved rural child hero of Jules
enard's story. The next year he played *Le Petit*
oi (The Little King), and resumed royalty in
938 in *L'Education du Prince* (The Education of
e Prince), with leads in other classics like

Sans Famille (1934, The Homeless) and *Le Petit*
Chose (1938, Little What's-His-Name), as well
as a small part in *Un Carnet de Bal* (1937, A
Dance Card), in his six-year film career. During
the war Lynen joined the French Resistance,
and was captured and executed by the Nazis –
who had also, shortly before, murdered the
marvellous old Jewish actor Harry Baur, his
father in *Poil de Carotte*.

Little girl found
The year of 1932 saw the arrival on the
Hollywood scene of the most famous little girl
star in cinema history. Shirley Temple (b.1928)
was the moppet to end all moppets – and end
them she did. Though boys had always hogged
the best parts, plenty of sweet little girls had
graced the screen since the 1890s, and some –
like Helen Badgley ('the Thanhouser Kidlet'),
Baby Marie Osborne and Baby Peggy Montgomery – had briefly become Darlings of the
Nation. But Temple had the luck to arrive at
exactly the right moment, the first brand-new
child prodigy of the talkies. In fact, she and the
cinema uttered their first sounds almost
simultaneously.

Having started to attend dancing lessons at
the age of two – Shirley's parents always
insisted that they had never planned on a film
career for her – she was spotted by a studio
scout for the Educational Film Corporation,
who were looking for tiny-tot protagonists for
a projected series called Baby Burlesks
(1932–33). As the name suggests, these were
movie skits performed by infants, and Shirley,
who landed the female lead, would find herself
being squired in them by, for instance, a knee-
high man-about-town in top hat and nappy.
Agonizing titles included *Kid'n Hollywood*
(Shirley was the 'Incomparable More Legs
Sweetrick': yes, she impersonated Dietrich),
Polly-Tix in Washington, and *Pie Covered*
Wagon. However blush-making these capers
may have been, Educational went ahead with

Top, far left: during the filming of Captain
January (1936) *Shirley Temple was troubled
by the loss of her baby teeth. Top left: between
takes on* Now and Forever (1935) *Gary
Cooper taught Shirley, whom he nicknamed
'Wigglebritches', to draw. Above left and top:
early two-reeler roles as 'La Belle Diaperina' in*
Glad Rags to Riches *and as 'More Legs
Sweetrick' in* Kid'n Hollywood. *Centre: in
Ford's* Wee Willie Winkie McLaglen, *as a soft-
hearted sergeant, was continually reduced to
tears by Shirley's antics. Above: an older
Shirley in* Since You Went Away (1944)
with Claudette Colbert and Jennifer Jones

a further series called Frolics of Youth (1933–34). Short kiddie films were two a penny at this time, and there was nothing so far to suggest that a star was being born. As mentioned earlier, Shirley was even given the brush-off by Our Gang. She made half a dozen small appearances in feature films between 1932 and 1934. In one of these, *Stand Up and Cheer* (1934), she was engaged to sing a song, 'Baby Take a Bow'. It caught everyone's fancy, and so did her performance in a much fatter part in *Little Miss Marker* soon afterwards. By the end of 1934, after three more parts of growing importance, stardom – in *Bright Eyes* – had arrived. Over the next three years she starred in ten pictures and was the Number One Box Office Attraction of the English-speaking world. By 1940, when her career at last faltered, she had earned about $3 million in some thirty films – roughly double Jackie Cooper's earnings. (Though it's worth remembering that Jackie Coogan a decade or so earlier was said to have made, allowing for inflation, a larger sum with only 20 films.)

Little Miss Hollywood

Miss Temple was certainly a phenomenon. How could it be accounted for? True, she was an exceptionally pretty child, of great charm and winsomeness – but then so are many child actors. She was highly intelligent (as her later career as a diplomat confirmed). So, again, are many child actors. She danced and sang, but not much better than average. She hadn't half the personality of Coogan, or the histrionic talent of Cooper – yet she was the hottest property in Hollywood during the middle and late Thirties. Why?

The titles of her films give the clue. Roughly half of the fifteen vehicles of 1935–39 contained the emotive word 'little', or 'wee', or even 'littlest': *The Little Colonel, Our Little Girl, The Littlest Rebel* (all 1935), *Poor Little Rich Girl* (1936), *Wee Willie Winkie* (1937), *Little Miss Broadway* (1938), *The Little Princess* (1939). Other titles included *Curly Top* (1935) and *Dimples* (1936). You were invited to go gooey

even before the movie started. It was a direct assault on the soft underbelly of the world's emotions, a blatant manipulation of what psychologists might call the *Aaah!-Effekt*. It evoked the low, abject moan of motherliness that can arise even from strong men caught off their guard by a gurgling baby or fluffy kitten. Shirley was *cute*: the word might have been coined for her. She didn't need to be a great actor, or singer, or dancer: just the sight of her *trying* to do any of these was enough to make her public chuckle happily and murmur, 'Oh, the little *pet*'. They loved to see her pout and toss her curls, or frown and wag a tiny finger and say, in effect, 'You naughty, *naughty* adult!' Like child movie actors from the dawn of time, she played the little guardian angel, laughingly comforting the downcast and reconciling the estranged; but she did it in the full, pristine glory of sound, and the impact of that, plus her divine comeliness, was devastating.

Now that all the ballyhoo of Shirley-mania is history, one can enjoy her films as the amazing period-pieces they are – products, however minor, of Hollywood in its full confident prime. But by the Forties her public was losing interest; she wasn't small enough to evoke the *Aaah!-Effekt* any more. As one attractive Hollywood teenager among many, she made another dozen or so films before retiring in 1949 and devoting herself to more serious matters.

Little girls lost

During her heyday, of course, Shirley Temple had several hopeful would-be challengers, promoted with pathetically short-lived energy. Warners imported a clever little English girl of similar age, Sybil Jason, who had mild success in a handful of films. England also produced a stilted tot called Binkie Stuart. France offered Gaby Triquet and Germany Traudl Stark. None clicked more than locally. In America, two delightful and talented girls, Bonita Granville and Edith Fellows, were no threat as they were five years older than Temple and did most

Above left: from the moment Jane Withers asked Santa Claus for a machine-gun in Bright Eyes, *she was destined to become the biggest brat in the movies. The little girls Jane played were definitely not very nice – but by 1937 films like* The Holy Terror *had made her the sixth most popular box-office star in America. Above:* Rainbow on the River *(1936) was one of the sugary musicals made by Bobby Breen. Bobby's film career was short-lived and he eventually became a night-club singer. Top: the German boy star Rolf Wenkhaus as Emil in the 1931 version of* Emil and the Detectives, *the story of a group of schoolboys who track down a thief with no cooperation from the police*

of their work between the ages of nine and 13 – the age at which Temple was later to run out of steam. The only other small girl to build up a real following was Jane Withers (b.1926), a tomboy of formidable temperament, who was first seen as a brute of a child in contrast to the angelic Shirley in *Bright Eyes* (1934). From 1935 to 1940, Withers made more films than Temple – not such chromium-plated ones, to be sure, but a lot of fun.

By the end of the Thirties the great period of child stars was over. Cooper, Bartholomew and Temple had faded in turn – though Rooney was doing nicely out of his prolonged adolescence. In Europe, most of the best performances came from children who were not stars and made no career: Rolf Wenkhaus in *Emil und die Detektive* (1931, *Emil and the Detectives*), Alyosha Lyarsky in *The Childhood of Maxim Gorki* (1938). No more major American child stars emerged. A nondescript singing lad called Bobby Breen warbled his way through a few dire musicals. Trumpet-playing Bennie Bartlett tried and failed to be a second Rooney. Intelligent little Virginia Weidler gave pleasure without threatening to be a star. The future lay with Roddy McDowall, Margaret O'Brien, Elizabeth Taylor, Bobby Driscoll, Dean Stockwell and a few other fine troupers. There were to be no more child deities – and a good thing too.

JOHN HOLMSTROM

Family viewing

Dream daughters, model fathers and idealized all-American families were box-office favourites for a generation of filmgoers and their children

In the mid-Thirties Hollywood was only dimly aware that World War II was just around the corner, and that an even greater menace called television was to threaten its existence after the war. Consequently the phenomenon of family cinema-going was, perhaps for the last time, a factor to be reckoned with in the film industry. Louis B. Mayer, a 'family man' even among movie moguls, once asked rhetorically:

'What will people say about Louis B. Mayer if he puts his name on a picture he's ashamed to let his family see?'

As TV companies were to discover later, family viewing was big business; what's more it meant that film producers could comfortably keep on the right side of the rigorous requirements of the Production Code and the strident demands of the Catholic Legion of Decency.

One obvious approach to dealing with the Catholic lobby was to have a priest for a hero. In a most improbable piece of casting, Spencer Tracy played a priest in *San Francisco* (1936) – up to this point he had been playing convicts, gangsters and con men. It was a powerful performance that earned Tracy his first Oscar nomination and set the pattern for his playing of the saintly Father Flanagan in *Boys Town* (1938). *San Francisco* had everything: Clark Gable at his rugged best as a gambling, brawling saloon-keeper, whose final reformation in no way affects one's enjoyment of his wicked career; Jeanette MacDonald's silvery voice putting over a memorable theme song; and the climactic earthquake, a triumph of the art of special effects.

Boys Town was a sentimental but effective account of how a dedicated priest who believes that there is no such thing as a 'bad' boy runs a home for juvenile delinquents. The chief delinquent was

played by the mercurial Mickey Rooney – then 16 but short in stature and ideally suited to go on playing juvenile roles well into his adolescence. Rooney was one of many highly talented American screen children whose films provided much of the popular fare for family audiences. Child stars were nothing new, of course, and had always been an essential ingredient of 'family pictures'. Mary Pickford was perhaps the most famous child star of the silent era, but Rooney and Jackie Cooper were the outstanding boy stars of the Thirties, with Jackie Searl often in close support as the sneak or sissy who was a necessary foil.

Among the little girls Shirley Temple reigned supreme. A fully-fledged star at five, she had a range of talents that has tended to be obscured by the saccharine image created for her by largely cynical critics. Her foil, as a mischievous and sometimes unpleasant child, was Jane Withers, but Bonita Granville was an even more remarkable performer of nasty little girls as her portrayal of the malevolent talebearer in *These Three* (1936) attested.

In the late Thirties MGM brought forward two young girls, both exceptionally talented musically. Judy Garland, curiously enough, was less successful at first, despite the hit she made in *The Wizard of Oz* (1939), but Deanna Durbin, dropped by MGM and taken up by Universal, became a box-office phenomenon – especially in Britain – from her very first film, *Three Smart Girls* (1937).

Deanna had a light, remarkably controlled soprano voice and a repertoire of popular classics. In *One Hundred Men and a Girl* (1937) she helped make so-called serious music more popular. But her singing would not have done the trick had she not had an exceptionally likeable personality. What really sold her to the public was the wholesome charm which made her every parent's favourite dream daughter.

As might be expected *Three Smart Girls* spawned a sequel – *Three Smart Girls Grow Up* (1939). Both

Top: the screen debut of Deanna Durbin, a teenage starlet whom parents and children idolized. Above: like recent disaster films, San Francisco had its share of song and romance. Left: Joseph Breen of the Catholic Legion of Decency. Below: the equally influential Judge Hardy and family whose screen lives began in 1937

PRODUCTION CODE CHIEF AT HOME

Herewith appears the latest photographic recording of Mr. Joseph I. Breen, director of the Production Code Administration, the motion picture industry's response to the Legion of Decency, pictured with his family at their residence in Hollywood. This is evidence enough that Mr. Breen may be considered an authority of experience on the requirements of a typical, healthy and lively American family, running the whole scale of ages represented in the motion picture audience. Left to right, seated: Natalie, Frances, Tommy, Helene; standing: James, Mr. and Mrs. Breen, Joseph.

Top: the Lane sisters and Gale Page played Claude Rains' dutiful Four Daughters *but the real sensation of the film was John Garfield in his screen debut. Top right: J.M. Barrie's literary classic* Quality Street *was an ideal vehicle for Hepburn and made for perfect family viewing. Centre right:* Daughters Courageous *starred the cast of* Four Daughters: *here they played an entirely different family but Garfield was back as the juvenile lead. Bottom right: Cukor's* Little Women *was not as saccharine as audiences might have expected. Above: David O. Selznick's production of* Tom Sawyer – *a typical example of a popular classic transferred to the screen. Right: Maureen O'Sullivan, Freddie Bartholomew and Edna May Oliver in* David Copperfield

were good examples of what exhibitors and distributors referred to as the 'family film', aimed specifically to appeal to the family audience. What perhaps lay behind the wish to identify with and follow the adventures of a desirable family group was a need for reassurance about traditional values in a changing world. More recent examples of the same tendency are the TV and radio soap operas like The Waltons in America or The Archers in Britain.

The Three Smart Girls films were directed by Henry Koster and featured Deanna as the youngest of three sisters. In the first she reconciles her estranged parents and in the second she helps to marry off her older sisters. Plot, however, is less important to these movies than the freshness and vitality of the girls, the support of a strong cast and the judicious blend of popular and classical songs.

A rather similar and appropriately titled 'family' series was launched in *Four Daughters* (1938). Featuring the attractive Lane sisters (Lola, Rosemary, and Priscilla) and Gale Page as the daughters of a musician, the film was also notable for the debut of John Garfield, who made a big impression as a poor boy with a chip on his shoulder. This and two of the sequels. *Daughters Courageous* (1939) and *Four Wives* (1939), were made by Michael Curtiz. Both these sequels shared the virtues of the original film but the next, William Keighley's *Four Mothers* (1940), was not able to sustain the momentum.

What all the films had in common was a thorough-going endorsement of the notion of family; the fact too, that stories were located in small-town, middle-America contributed to the image of a homogenized society based on traditional family values.

The most successful family series ever was undoubtedly the Hardy Family, featured in 14 films between 1937 and 1945. Judge Hardy, played originally by Lionel Barrymore but later by Lewis Stone, was a justice of the utmost probity given to having heart-to-heart chats with his volatile son Andy. As played by Mickey Rooney, Andy was inevitably larger than life and twice as natural. If these films seem over-sweet today, it still does not prevent them from being entertaining for audiences not entirely corroded by cynicism.

Literary classics were another cornerstone of family entertainment in the Thirties and provided a further extension of the daughters, wives and families themes already noted. The works of authors like Charles Dickens, Louisa May Alcott and Frances Hodgson Burnett suggest sentimentality, but in the hands of sensitive directors like George Cukor and John Cromwell the authors were well served; as Cukor himself said, 'If you really respect a work, you must respect the weaknesses, the vagaries, as well as the strength'.

Neither he nor Cromwell believed in tidying up a story to fit modern concepts and their versions are consequently as timeless as the originals. Cukor has said that he had thought of *Little Women* as a story little girls read:

'When I came to read it I was startled. It's not sentimental or saccharine, but very strong-minded, full of character, and a wonderful picture of New England family life. It's full of that admirable New England sternness, about sacrifice and austerity.'

Cukor's film of *Little Women* (1933) was equally vigorous, thanks largely to Katharine Hepburn's wonderfully fresh and tender portrayal of Jo. The director went on to film *David Copperfield* (1935), in collaboration with David O. Selznick. It was the same producer who set John Cromwell to work on *Little Lord Fauntleroy* (1936) and *The Prisoner of Zenda* (1937). From its reputation as a legendary tear-jerker *Little Lord Fauntleroy* emerged, under Cromwell's careful guidance, as a sharply observed and humorous story whose hero, played by Freddie Bartholomew, was a natural and likeable child.

Cromwell's version of *The Prisoner of Zenda* is one of the great swashbucklers of all time and it provided Douglas Fairbanks Jr with a fine romantic part.

It was Selznick again who produced one of the best Mark Twain adaptations: *The Adventures of Tom Sawyer* (1938), directed by Norman Taurog (who had made a version of *Huckleberry Finn* with Jackie Coogan back in 1931). This version, the second in Hollywood during the decade, starred Tommy Kelly and Jackie Moran and had a strong cast of character players including Victor Jory as Injun Joe. The film owed much to the art direction of William Cameron Menzies and reflected once again Selznick's tireless quest for the perfect team in each production. Indeed it is a notable fact – borne out by MGM's *A Tale of Two Cities* (1935) in which Ronald Colman gave the definitive performance of Sidney Carton – that wherever several versions exist of the same classic novel it is almost always the Selznick version that is best remembered.

Costume drama that revolved around a family situation was reliable family-audience fare. Katharine Hepburn – who had begun her film career as a very modern young woman – was a familiar and popular star of many such pictures, following her success in *Little Women*. She was also featured in two adaptations from stories by J.M. Barrie, produced by Pandro S. Berman for RKO. She was radiant as the wild and wilful Babbie in *The Little Minister* (1934) and, in a very different mood, gave a restrained and elegant account of the ageing spinster in *Quality Street* (1937, directed by George Stevens). Stevens also directed her in another of her best characterizations – that of the funny but

pathetic small-town snob in Booth Tarkington's *Alice Adams* (1935).

Literary adaptations were safe bets: they had already succeeded in another medium, they were free from copyright at a time when studios were feeling the pinch, and they were respectable. This meant that the whole family could enjoy them and the self-appointed guardians of America's morals would approve of them. In a similar vein the stories of the lives of famous men and women provided good doses of moral uplift. The success of these 'biopics' in the Thirties may be compared with the historical biographies so popular on television today. *The Story of Louis Pasteur* (1935), *The Life of Emile Zola* (1937) and *Juarez* (1939) – three excellent biographies – were all directed by William Dieterle whose reputation largely *rests* on his screen biographies. The careers of famous statesmen were also reckoned to be acceptable subjects for audiences of

all ages and in the course of *Disraeli* (1929), starring George Arliss and *Clive of India* (1935), starring Ronald Colman, the vital ingredient of adventure was never overlooked. Towards the end of the decade Hollywood got around to dramatizing the lives of American statesmen. Henry Fonda, for example, played Lincoln in Ford's *Young Mr Lincoln* (1939) and in Cromwell's follow-up *Abe Lincoln in Illinois* (1940).

In the final analysis Hollywood's formula for building the loyalty of family audiences was to base its films on happy families, famous lives or famous books, often scaled down to the comfortable, familiar environment of the all-purpose small town. It was as though Alexander Graham Bell (played by Don Ameche in the 1939 film), Tom Sawyer and the Hardy family all grew up and lived in the same town: a place that was as familiar an image of America as the idyllic village was of England, and a place where the Hollywood moguls may have imagined their audiences to live.

BRENDA DAVIES

Top left: The Story of Alexander Graham Bell *was so popular that for awhile people referred to the telephone as 'the Ameche' after the film's star.* Don Ameche. *Left:* Ronald Colman *expands the British Empire in* Clive of India. *Above:* Colman *was at his peak in* The Prisoner of Zenda – *the ideal schoolboy story-hero. Below:* Jack Conway *directs* Colman *and* Elizabeth Allan *in MGM's screen version of Dickens'* A Tale of Two Cities

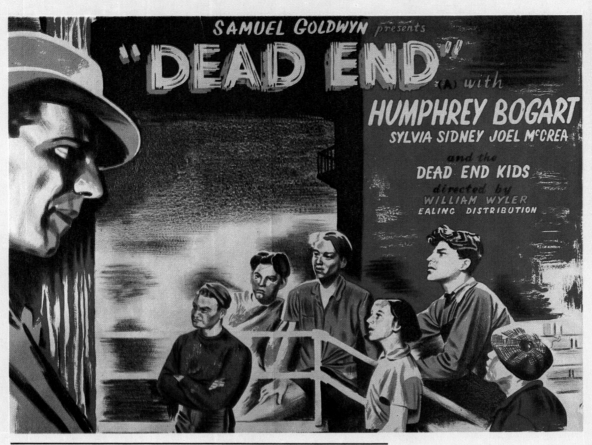

Directed by William Wyler, 1937

Prod: Samuel Goldwyn. **ass prod:** Merritt Hulburd. **sc:** Lillian Hellman, based on the play by Sidney Kingsley. **photo:** Gregg Toland. **ed:** Daniel Mandell. **art dir:** Richard Day, Julie Heron. **cost:** Omar Kiam. **mus dir:** Alfred Newman. **sd:** Frank Maher. **ass dir:** Eddie Bernoud. **r/t:** 93 minutes. New York premiere, 24 August 1937.

Cast: Sylvia Sidney (*Drina*), Joel McCrea (*Dave*), Humphrey Bogart (*'Baby Face' Martin*), Wendy Barrie (*Kay*), Claire Trevor (*Francey*), Allen Jenkins (*Hunk*), Marjorie Main (*Mrs Martin*), Billy Halop (*Tommy*), Huntz Hall (*Dippy*), Bobby Jordan (*Angel*), Leo Gorcey (*Spit*) Gabriel Dell (*T.B.*), Bernard Punsly (*Milty*), Charles Peck (*Philip*), Minor Watson (*Mr Griswold*), James Burke (*Mulligan*), Ward Bond (*doorman*), Elizabeth Risdon (*Mrs Connell*), Esther Dale (*Mrs Fenner*), George Humbert (*Mr Pascagli*), Marcelle Corday (*governess*), Charles Halton (*Whitey*), Donald Barry (*intern*).

Dead End was adapted from Sydney Kingsley's controversial and successful play of the same name which ran for 700 performances on Broadway. After seeing it, Sam Goldwyn was determined to secure the film rights – which eventually cost the then record sum of $165,000.

The play concerns the brutalizing effect of life in the slums, and in particular how adolescents easily become trapped into crime as the sole available means of bettering themselves.

Goldwyn was probably not so much moved by a burning sense of social conscience as by an eagerness to secure a 'prestige' property. He soon assembled a 'prestige' cast, retaining only Marjorie Main and the Dead End Kids from the Broadway production. Joel McCrea, then under contract to Goldwyn, took the lead role; from Warner Brothers Goldwyn borrowed Humphrey Bogart who had just scored a great success in *The Petrified Forest* (1936); and from Walter Wanger he obtained Sylvia Sidney, star of Lang's *Fury* and Hitchcock's *Sabotage* (both 1936).

Lillian Hellman's script made some changes to the original piece. A central character of the play, a crippled, bitter artist, was metamorphosed into the poor but idealistic Dave – one of the 'moral guardians' of Dead End. Certain taboo screen topics, such as the exact nature of the non-marital relationship of Dave's sweetheart Kay with a wealthy businessman, and the fact that Martin's girlfriend Francey has syphilis, are only vaguely alluded to. More damaging was the decision to adhere to the play's rigid time structure – one day. Within the space of 24 hours, far too much happens to far too many people to be wholly believable. The pace of the film makes the slums of Dead End appear exciting places to live in, instead of dreary and depressing as they really are.

The director William Wyler wanted to shoot the picture in real New York locations, but Goldwyn insisted that a massive studio set be built, and supplied $300,000 for the purpose. This was the first of several arguments the pair had over realism during the making of the film. Arthur Marx wrote in his biography of Goldwyn:

'Sam rebelled against having too much realism in *Dead End*, just as he did in all his pictures. It was one of his quirks, perhaps a hangover from the squalor of his youth, that made him believe that picture audiences demanded a certain amount of glamour even though the story might call for the characters to dress in rags and look dirty and the background to be ugly and decrepit.'

Despite Goldwyn's interference, the combination of Wyler's direction, Richard Day's set, Gregg Toland's photography with its inventive use of angles and light and shadow, and the performances of the cast, satisfied contemporary reviewers. The *New York Times* commented:

'*Dead End* deserves a place among the important motion pictures of the year for its stout and well-presented reiteration of the social protest that was the theme of the original.'

The opening shots of the film, using titles to back up the images, reveal a stark contrast between the tall apartment blocks of the rich (attracted by the picturesque waterfront scenery) and the broken-down tenements of the poor. Forced by economic circumstances to be forever outside looking in, the Kids' spontaneity and vitality is coloured by resentment against the better-off and their lackeys – the doorman and governess. The Kids are not unduly sentimentalized. Documentary film-maker Basil Wright noted in the *Spectator*:

'Each one of them, in looks and character, is unerringly and absolutely the real thing.'

Although tough and 'street-wise', the Kids are not all bad – but they quickly succumb to the influence of gangster 'Baby Face' Martin. He appears to be living proof that crime pays, invalidating Dave and Drina's belief that honesty is the best policy.

Martin's choice of crime as a way of life results in the breakdown of every relationship he holds dear. His mother rejects him, Francey disgusts him, and his neighbourhood (as represented by Dave) shoots him. Though Tommy is on the road to delinquency, Dave and Drina can still appeal to *his* active sense of relationship with others; they persuade him to give himself up to Mr Griswold. Having just witnessed the shoot-out and Tommy's flight and attempted revenge on Spit the squealer, we expect a conventional happy ending. But the film remains uncompromising. The influential Griswold (his brother is a judge) disregards his social responsibilities and uses the police to exact a revenge no different in essence from a gangland vendetta – he cannot forgive Tommy and his gang for roughing up his boy. He is quite prepared to ruin Tommy's future prospects.

Dave and Drina's faith in the social and moral virtues of honesty and mercy is shown to be in vain. Instead they are forced to pin their hopes on the reward money Dave gained by killing Martin in a fit of revengeful fury. This ending gives the film a quality of cynicism about American society unusual in a Hollywood feature of the time. It may explain the fact that although the picture was nominated for four Academy Awards it failed to win in any category.   ALASTAIR DOUGALL

Below: Wyler (seated) directs a scene with the Dead End Kids

A gang of slum kids roam Dead End, a street near New York's East River (1). Their leader, Tommy, has been raised by his sister Drina. She is in love with Dave (2), an unemployed architect, but he has fallen for Kay (3), who is being kept by a rich businessman in a nearby fashionable apartment.

The infamous gangster 'Baby Face' Martin returns to his old neighbourhood with his henchman Hunk (4). Dave recognizes him but promises silence if Martin leaves soon. Martin, his face changed by plastic surgery, is on the run and wishes to see his mother and Francey, an old girlfriend, before he leaves town. His mother spurns him (5), and he is horrified to find that Francey has become a prostitute.

The Kids pounce on Philip Griswold, a rich boy, and steal his watch. His father catches Tommy who threatens him with a knife in order to escape. Griswold sets the police after him and Tommy goes into hiding.

Martin plans to kidnap Philip, but when Dave threatens to expose him to the police, Martin knifes Dave, who is left for dead. However, Dave is only wounded. He knocks out Hunk, takes his gun, and chases and shoots Martin (6), thereby winning a large reward.

Spit, one of the Kids, is caught by police and 'squeals' on Tommy. Tommy catches him, but Dave persuades Tommy to forgive Spit (7) and to throw himself on Griswold's mercy. Griswold turns a deaf ear to their pleas and hands Tommy over to the law (8). Dave, who has come to realize that he and Kay are not suited, promises to pay a good lawyer to save Tommy from reform school and an inevitable life of crime. Dave and Drina decide to start a new life together far away from Dead End.

Meet Me in St Louis

Meet Me in St Louis, an adaptation of Sally Benson's memoirs of American provincial life at the turn of the century, was much praised at the time of its release – during World War II – as a reassuring evocation of an era in American history when innocence rather than confusion reigned supreme. And, indeed, with its radiant, 'chocolate box' colours, its vivid sense of period and its preoccupation with the fineries and fripperies that surround the Smiths as they busy themselves doing nothing, the film has the look of a bourgeois notion of paradise.

Following a dissolve from a greeting card-like illustration of the Smith house in summer (which establishes the formal division of the film into four acts, each corresponding to a season), the family is introduced in the kitchen of their home. Tomato ketchup is being prepared and, in swift succession, the members of the family taste and then flavour to their liking the bubbling concoction. Their 'dispute' is trivial, but the point it makes is clear: each of the Smiths is concerned at every point to make the world anew in his or her own image

in order to be free. Another particularly fine example of this is the lengthy sequence after the party when John Truett helps Esther turn out the lights to create an appropriate atmosphere for the beginning of their courtship. As they move through the rooms, director Vincente Minnelli's fluid camera captures the changing ambience of the environment while the hesitant lovers make the Smith household their own.

The world of *Meet Me in St Louis*, unlike that of either Minnelli's more free-flowing musicals or his social dramas, is both harmonious and static. Nevertheless, the friendly rivalry for attention that characterizes the relations between the members of the family, which reaches its boiling point with Mr Smith's decision to move them all to New York, is real – and the story has the possibility of unhappiness for all its characters. This tension within the film can be separated into two strands: one is the drive for self-gratification, represented by Esther (played by Judy Garland, whose exuberant performance was presumably partly a reflection of

her burgeoning love affair with Minnelli); the other is the possibility of real pain, represented by Tootie (Margaret O'Brien).

From the beginning, with the impromptu opening performance of the title song, Esther's dreams come effortlessly true. The mythical boy-next-door appears on cue, is serenaded and immediately declares his love with all the evasions and embarrassments that social conventions require. When it seems that he will be unable to join Esther and her friends on a trip to the site of the World's Fair, her vigorous rendition of 'The Trolley Song' brings him running from nowhere to catch the trolley just in time. Finally, John proposes to Esther before the projected move to New York is cancelled; even though they will be temporarily separated their happiness is assured. By way of contrast, it is only after Mr Smith has told his family that he has decided to stay in St Louis that Rose's more problematic romance reaches a happy resolution.

If Esther's part in the story is a straightforward one, Tootie's is highly complex. The dreams and

4

1

5

6

Directed by Vincente Minnelli, 1944
Prod co: MGM. **prod:** Arthur Freed. **sc:** Fred Finklehoffe, Irving Brecher, based on the book by Sally Benson. **photo:** George Folsey. **col:** Technicolor. **ed:** Albert Akst. **art dir:** Cedric Gibbons, Lemuel Ayers, Jack Martin Smith, Edwin B. Willis, Paul Huldschinsky. **cost:** Irene Sharaff. **mus dir:** George Stoll. **mus adapt:** Roger Edens. **songs:** Hugh Martin, Ralph Blane; Kerry Mills, Andrew B. Sterling; Nacio Herb Brown, Arthur Freed; Bob Cole. **chor:** Charles Walters. **r/t:** 113 minutes.
Cast: Judy Garland (*Esther Smith*), Mary Astor (*Mrs Smith*), Leon Ames (*Mr Smith*), Margaret O'Brien (*Tootie Smith*), Lucille Bremer (*Rose Smith*), Tom Drake (*John Truett*), Marjorie Main (*Katie*), Harry Davenport (*Grandpa*), June Lockhart (*Lucille Ballard*), Henry H. Daniels Jr (*Lon Smith Jr*), Joan Carroll (*Agnes Smith*), Hugh Marlowe (*Colonel Darly*).

Three of the delightful musical numbers from the film: 'The Cakewalk' (left), 'The Trolley Song' (far left) and 'Have Yourself a Merry Little Christmas' (below left), all with Judy Garland

aspirations of the rest of the family are thoroughly comfortable and conventional, but Tootie's desires are uncontrollable and chilling (the dominant subject of her conversation is death) and, as she is caught between childhood and adolescence, they are unchecked by social conventions and adult awareness. Accordingly, at the party that Esther hopes to end with a kiss from John without seeming to be too forward, Tootie, when she accompanies her in 'The Cakewalk', flaunts and mocks the sexuality Esther is afraid to admit. Similarly Halloween for Tootie is not an empty social ritual but a deadly desperate venture in which she must overcome her fearful visions of demons. This is underlined by Minnelli's treatment of it as an almost Expressionistic sequence in contrast to his naturalistic treatment of the film's musical numbers.

Meet Me in St Louis' most stunning moment comes when the film's happy ending is in sight (John has just proposed to Esther); just before it comes to pass, Minnelli offers a final and extreme glimpse of the possibility of unhappiness in Tootie's desperate slaying of the 'father-figure' of the snowman. But although Tootie's fantasies and actions are the ultimate expression of the hopes and fears of the family, she is also a child and can be comforted by Esther singing 'Have Yourself a Merry Little Christmas' to her, rather as a mother might ease her daughter's fears.

The crisis averted with the decision to stay in St Louis, the Smith family returns to its contented way of life before the Spring epilogue when they celebrate the presence of the World's Fair – in Esther's words, 'in our own back yard'. Thus at the end of the film everybody is happy again, but only because they have all got their own way.

PHIL HARDY

It is the summer of 1903 in St Louis. At the home of Alonso and Anna Smith and their five children, tomato ketchup is being made and everyone expresses an opinion about it, including Grandpa (1). Rose and Esther, the older daughters, are anxious about their beaux: Esther (2) wants John Truett, the boy-next-door; Rose's boy calls from New York but Father is cross and slams the phone down (3). At brother Lon's party Esther and Tootie perform 'The Cakewalk' and afterwards Esther manages to see John alone. On a visit to the fairground to see the World's Fair preparations she sings 'The Trolley Song' and continues to captivate John.

Autumn. On Halloween Tootie and Agnes join the local children (4) in 'murdering' the neighbours – and Tootie performs the supreme act of 'killing' the most dreaded neighbour alone. Later she is hurt (5) and accuses John Truett of beating her. Esther attacks him but then learns it was a mistake. Later, to the family's dismay, Father announces that he is moving them to New York (6).

Winter. The move draws near. After the Christmas Eve dance John proposes to Esther and is accepted. Tootie is still upset by the prospect of the move and smashes up her snowmen, but Esther comforts her (7). Father relents and announces that the move is off.

Spring. The World's Fair comes to St Louis and Esther and John (8) and the rest of the family join in the celebrations.

3

7

8

In the first feature he directed, *La Bataille du Rail* (1946, The Battle of the Railway Workers), René Clément attempted to portray with documentary realism an episode from the French Resistance. *Jeux Interdits* (Forbidden Games) is also set in France during World War II and shows a concern for authentic period detail. The time covered – as is revealed through the close-up of a newspaper headline, topical allusions by the characters, the date on a label around a child's neck – is five days in 1940, from June 16 to June 20 – the moment when Marshal Pétain took over as premier from Reynaud and, faced with the collapse of his country's army, began to sue for peace. This was the period when the roads of France were crowded with civilians fleeing the invading German army and offering easy targets for the bombs and machine-guns of the Luftwaffe.

The opening sequence of *Jeux Interdits* depicts such an attack by Messerschmitts on a column of refugees, in a manner and on a scale that recall the mood and presentation of some heroic set-pieces in *La Bataille du Rail*. But the film as a whole is a very different work. None of the main adult characters here shows the bravery displayed by the railwaymen in the earlier feature – indeed, one of them, Francis Gouard, is a deserter who has no patriotic sentiments and no feeling of shame. This is not, however, to suggest that, having portrayed the courage of his countrymen who resisted the Germans, Clément now wanted to present the other side of the coin.

For the most part *Jeux Interdits* is focused on the activities of a five-year-old girl, orphaned by the air-raid depicted in the initial scenes, and an eleven-year-old boy from a peasant family. In fact, despite the accuracy with which it is portrayed, the war serves mainly as a powerful and dramatic context in which to set a particular view of childhood.

It is made clear that neither of the children in *Jeux Interdits* is capable of fully understanding the idea of death. Paulette is shown to be astonished, but not really distressed, by the inert bodies of her slain parents. When the wife of her would-be rescuer tells her that her dog is dead, the little girl's repetition of the sentence suggests that it is the first time she has heard the word 'dead'. Michel, though older and consequently more knowledgeable, is nevertheless likewise incapable of comprehending the notion of death, as is revealed by the scenes showing his reactions to his brother's sudden demise: though initially taken aback by Paulette's asking if he is going to 'dig a hole' for Georges, he then finds it extremely difficult to suppress his giggles at the suggestion, while the adults in the family gaze in shock at the body of the deceased.

Such scenes show not the cruelty but the purity of children, and are handled with surprising humour. Moreover, the funereal games in which Michel and Paulette indulge are seen as a direct and innocent response to adult behaviour. As Clément made clear in an interview, the film was intended to illustrate a form of determinist philosophy:

'In *Jeux Interdits* I wanted to show the terrifying responsibility we adults have towards children for we must not forget that every one of our actions is an example for them to follow.'

In creating a cemetery for animals, in the first instance to provide company for the dead dog which was Paulette's favourite play-thing, the two children are merely translating into their own terms the actions they have observed in their elders. Given a world where adults in planes drop bombs on adults on the ground, it is not surprising that Michel, in emulation, drops his sharp-pointed pen on a cockroach. Given the rituals of the Christian church followed by their elders, it is not surprising that Paulette and Michel should wish to mouth prayers over the graves of the animals they have killed. Given the dishonesty and greed of the grown-ups around them, it is not surprising that the children should steal crosses to decorate their cemetery.

The adults in the film are seen to be shocked by the children's actions – as indeed were many contemporary critics! For Clément, however, Paulette and Michel cannot be condemned for they have no in-built sense of right or wrong:

'Children waver between Good and Evil, making choices as a result of the behaviour they observe in us.'

It is, therefore, the adult world that is indicted in the film: its inhumanity revealed in the air-raid portrayed in the opening sequence; its hypocrisy strikingly illustrated by the ironically comic scenes of the fist-fight in the cemetery between Dollé and Gouard, each of whom considers the other to have committed an act of blasphemy. Ultimately, this grown-up world destroys the children's innocence, for Michel's father breaks his word and hands over Paulette to the Red Cross. As she waits among a crowd of people to be shipped off to another part of France, she hears someone calling the name 'Michel'. Looking around in vain for the boy, she suddenly becomes aware of the loss not only of her friend but of her parents and calls out desperately for her mother.

The comment on human behaviour which the director claimed to be making is based on a rather simplistic determinism that is not rigourously applied, but the film happily transcends the intended sociological message. Beautifully shot and lit, wittily scripted, accompanied by a haunting piece of music and, above all, superbly acted by the two children, *Jeux Interdits* is a charmingly humorous and intensely moving film which succeeds in implanting in the mind of the spectator an unforgetable vision of childhood innocence.

ALISTAIR WHYTE

24

Les Jeux Interdit

3

4

7

8

It is June 1940. A country road in France is thronged with civilians fleeing the invading German army. Suddenly. enemy aircraft attack the column of refugees, killing, among others, the parents of five-year-old Paulette (1). Bewildered, the little girl cradles in her arms the body of her dead dog. When the wife of a would-be rescuer hurls it into a nearby river, Paulette recovers it and in doing so meets eleven-year-old Michel Dollé (2), who takes her home to his parents' small-holding.

Paulette is too young to understand death and appears to know nothing of Catholicism but, inspired by remarks of the adults in her new-found family, she decides to bury her dog. Next day, Michel discovers the little girl digging a hole in an old mill (3) and tells her that the dead are buried in cemeteries so that they can keep each other company. He promises to make one for her. Taking the body of a mole from an owl's nest, he makes a grave for it next to that of the dog.

In the attic room of the Dollé home, Michel makes wooden crosses for their graveyard (4) and teaches Paulette prayers. Meanwhile his older brother, Georges, who has been kicked by a startled horse, dies of an internal haemorrhage to the surprise of all the family.

Michel steals, and presumably kills, two chicks to add to their cemetery and also removes three of the wooden crosses from his brother's hearse. When questioned by his father (5) he blames the next-door neighbour, Gouard, whom his father hates and whose deserter son is having an affair with Michel's older sister Berthe.

After the funeral service for Georges, Michel attempts to steal the cross on the wall of the church (6) but is caught and punished by the parish priest. Undeterred, the children go to the cemetery that night and steal 14 crosses (7), including the one from Georges' grave. As a result Dollé and Gouard have a fight in the cemetery (8) the following day, but the priest suspects that the real culprit is Michel. The police arrive to take Paulette to the Red Cross. The boy agrees to reveal the location of the crosses when his father promises that Paulette can stay in the family for good. But Dollé breaks his word and hands over the little girl to the police (9). Michel destroys the cemetery that the children built. Paulette, at the Red Cross depot, on her own again (10), cries out for her dead mother.

Directed by René Clément, 1952
Prod co: Silver Films. **prod:** Robert Dorfmann. **sc:** Jean Aurenche, Pierre Bost, René Clément, François Boyer, from the novel by François Boyer. **photo:** Robert Juillard. **ed:** Robert Dwyre. **art dir:** Paul Bertrand. **mus:** Narciso Yepes. **sd:** Jacques Lebreton. **r/t:** 84 minutes. Released in the USA as *Forbidden Games*.
Cast: George Poujouly (*Michel Dollé*), Brigitte Fossey (*Paulette*), Amedée (*Francis Gouard*), Laurence Badie (*Berthe Dollé*), Suzanne Courtal (*Madame Dollé*), Lucien Hubert (*Monsieur Dollé*), Jacques Marin (*Georges Dollé*), Louis Sainteve (*the Curé*), Andre Wasley (*Monsieur Gouard*), Pierre Merovée (*Raymond Dollé*).

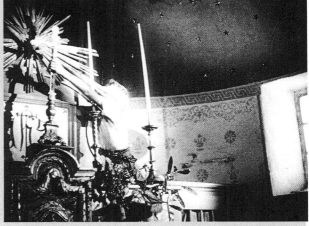
5

6

9

10

Teen dreams

Suddenly, in the mid-Fifties, there were teenagers everywhere, dancing to rock'n'roll music and dating at the drive-ins; up on the screen, the teenage hero acted out a generation's fantasies

The Fifties was that era when the cinema really discovered 'problems' – specifically problems of youth. Spurred on by newspaper headlines, filmmakers proceeded first to present, then to exploit and, by default, investigate the 'teen problem'. This process required that the movies assimilate contemporary events and attitudes, so that every fad and fetish of society served as raw material – grist to the mills of mythology.

The Fifties also saw the full integration of popular music into an evolving youth culture. It was a culture of full-blooded consumerism. In the public mind, the adjective 'teenage' referred to leisure, pleasure and conspicuous consumption. The teenagers' new music, rock'n'roll, symbolized a world of youth, caught up momentarily in hedonism and unrelated to adult interests. Rock'n'roll also brought with it a host of concepts and images that fired the public's ideas of youth: delinquency, adolescent gangs, motorcycle worship, ballroom-dance halls, jazz clubs, Melody Bars, Teddy Boys and similar phenomena.

Parents feared that the uncouth jungle music meant an end to the civilized order as they knew it. Of course, they were to be proved wrong as rock'n'roll became big business and, later, show business. Through its stars and principals, however, early rock'n'roll was aggressive in providing ideas of style that were exclusively teenage.

The young had always worshipped idols: Frank Sinatra, Johnny Ray, sports heroes and film stars. But now they had idols whose backgrounds, ages and interests they perceived as similar to their own. They sensed a whole culture of their own with a codified set of values clearly different from those of older generations. Participating in such a culture seemed a fitting rebellion against unreasonable, or merely conventional, ideas of how things should be experienced.

A commitment to enjoyment and consumer culture was in itself a statement against seriousness, drabness, 'adult' duties and responsibilities. And those professionals who dealt with the young (doctors, teachers, clergymen and social workers) feared what they interpreted as the absence of any public or community spirit on the part of the teenagers. The result of this anxiety was the image of a 'teenage jungle' as depicted by the media. A 1957 paperback called *The Teenage Jungle* gives an adequate description:

'Here is a frightful indictment of youthful crime and vice in the USA. It shows how the violent and sex-crazed teenage cult exists in a living nightmare of ruthlessness and depravity. These are the ordinary kids you read about every day of your life – ordinary, that is, until they shoot a store-keeper, assault a girl, torture a bum or wind up dead in a ditch.'

The aggressive manner, in which teenagers identified with one another, and the singularity and exclusivity of the teenage cult, quickly became bracketed with deviancy and delinquency in the view of the scandal-hungry media. The teenagers'

deliberate gestures of individuality, therefore, were interpreted as stances of defiance, aimed at their elders.

But in opposition to this view of the teenager there was the image of the pre-packaged teenager ready to be served up on the screen, in paperbacks and record stores. And the sentiments of the ordinary teenager in the Fifties were still very much a part of their period. The rhythms on the radio might have quickened but the emotional texture of the time had not. Like their parents, most middle-class teenagers were trusting and optimistic. What this meant in terms of the way they were represented in cinema was that film musicals incorporating rock'n'roll – rather like the music itself – often carried absurdly romantic lyrics and the 'teenpix', as the genre became known, often lumbered under abysmally stilted plots in an effort to reconcile new energies with traditional ideals.

The motion picture – which might appear to be a series of typical teenage happenings, but which was always framed, directed and marketed by adults – provided the mechanism for resolving the problems of being a teenager. Anticipation of everything that was new gave way to acceptance of things as they were. And, in the movies, acceptance meant happy endings. The teenager's naive crusade for abstracts like justice, freedom or individual dignity, could be portrayed and simultaneously merged with the comforts of the middle-class goal – conformity. If young people could be assimilated in this way they could be tacitly absolved from questioning the *status quo*.

Some of the musical films which evolved to cash in on rock'n'roll reflected this trend in their form as much as in content. They drew directly on the proscenium-arch tradition of the American musical which, by nature of its rigid division between stage and audience, could be described as a theatre of

Top: Tom Ewell and Jayne Mansfield in The Girl Can't Help It. *Frank Tashlin's garish but good-natured send-up of the rock'n'roll scene revolved around the dumb blonde's bid for rock stardom; despite the third-hand plot and older-generation stars, the film had more anarchic energy than all its imitators – and it had a line-up that included Fats Domino and Little Richard. Above: the inspiration for teen dreams and for most rock'n'roll movies was the hit single, though some – like Ray Peterson's 'Tell Laura I Love Her' – dealt in tragedies that many mainstream rock movies preferred to avoid*

Top right: the flash of steel in the 'teenage jungle': Bob Turnbull threatens Gary Clarke in Dragstrip Riot, which climaxed in a war between youth gangs. Top: similar, real-life battles were waged on the streets of New York; this news photo shows kids wearing protective body-shields. Centre: Sandra Dee in the title role of Gidget, every teenager's dream date. Above: Anne Neyland and Steve Terrell as teenage lovers in Motorcycle Gang

acceptance. Films as diverse as *Where the Boys Are* (1960), *West Side Story* (1961) and the early Elvis Presley epics all assume that the new, younger audience will automatically accept the old conventions and will swallow the hotted-up version of the so-called big production number – Hollywood's unwitting celebration of mindlessness.

The thrill of the star-vehicle musical remained undeniable: proof that the star could be fitted into an ordinary social perspective and could be sold at the box-office as a commodity to America's consumer class. The advent of the teenage idols of the Fifties – James Dean, Elvis, Sandra Dee – heralded youth's yearning to see the rite of stardom enacted over and over again. He or she symbolized the individual's rise not to riches – as might have been the case for the idols of the previous generation – but to popularity, social mobility and that state of absolute self-knowledge characterized by the adjective 'cool'.

Stardom was always double-edged. As well as confirming the collective aspirations of teenhood, stars also became part of an elite which put a distance between them and their fans and dramatized the worshipper's isolation and sneaking sense of unworthiness. The star was doomed to become an individual, isolated from his or her society.

Teenage idolatry had its origins in the pre-rock'n'roll era when jazz clubs, coffee bars and motorcycle gangs acted as a focus for the emerging teenage sensibility. In 1953 Marlon Brando appeared as Johnny, leader of the motor-bike gang the Black Rebels in *The Wild One*.

Two years later, *The Blackboard Jungle* (1955) featured Glenn Ford as a vocational schoolteacher trying to 'get through' to his New York City charges. The kids refer to him as 'Daddy-O' – one of the earliest commercial usages of the teenagers' 'heptalk' – and in the same year youth confronted adult incomprehension in *Rebel Without a Cause*.

The first big burst of rock films came in 1956 with *Rock Around the Clock*, directed by Sam Katzman and starring Bill Haley and the Comets. Katzman was to become a prolific producer of 'teenpix' none of which ever lost money. In 1961, less than a month after Chubby Checker hit the top of the record charts with 'The Twist', Katzman opened his movie *Twist Around the Clock* (1961) which starred Dion and The Marcels. Before the craze faded, he also managed to churn out *Don't Knock the Twist* (1962), featuring Chubby Checker again, this time with The Dovells and Gene Chandler.

Speed was of the essence in the manipulation of the 'teen market'. *Don't Knock the Rock* (1956) a sequel to *Rock Around the Clock*, was on the screen the same year as its predecessor. So was Frank

Tashlin's trail-blazing *The Girl Can't Help It* (1956) in which Fats Domino, Little Richard, Eddie Cochran and Nino Tempo lend support to a plot that revolved around Jayne Mansfield's attempts to become a singer.

Then, at the height of his celebrity, Elvis Presley made the classic *Jailhouse Rock* (1957), in which he played a good-kid-gone-wrong in a rags-to-riches saga. Here was real rock drama as Elvis, rehearsing in a recording studio, spontaneously decides to cut an upbeat number for a change. Another teenage idol was immortalized on screen in *The James Dean Story* (1957), co-directed by George W. George and Robert Altman. This posthumous documentary flopped at the box-office but Altman's other film of 1957, *The Delinquents*, had strong 'teen appeal' in its archetypal tale of a troubled teenager, his loving, but disapproving parents, a gang of local hoods, and a forbidden party on the edge of town. Like the voice-over narration of *The James Dean Story*, the disclaimers which frame *The Delinquents* have a familiar 'preaching' quality. Speaking about *The Delinquents* from the perspective of the Seventies Altman claimed:

'The violence was aimless, the result of restlessness and a feeling of "Let's just go in there and mess around".'

The film offered the same existential view of directionless youth as *Rebel Without a Cause*. In the notorious 'chicken-run' sequence, Jim asks Buzz 'Why do we do this then?' and Buzz replies 'You've gotta do something now, don't you?'

Towards the end of the decade, the wilder side of youth's aimlessness was being commercially cultivated by studios like American International Pictures. Two producers, Samuel Z. Arkoff and James H. Nicholson, had founded AIP with the aim of mounting 'teen appeal' packages which would portray American youth as decent rather than delinquent. The closely knit, family-style unit of directors, producers, writers and actors enabled AIP to minimize costs and production time on films. These movies were shot for next to nothing but their production costs were always equalled or surpassed by the amount poured into their promotion and for this reason they became known as 'exploitation movies'.

Of the many AIP producers and directors, the most brilliant was Roger Corman who produced for AIP *The Fast and the Furious* (1954), a road-racing epic with plenty of heptalk. Corman's most important youth movie of the period was, however, made for Allied Artists. Entitled *Teenage Doll* (1957), it was a moody picture with a well-paced plot and sympathy for teenage alienation. On a rainy street one night, the Black Widows (a girl gang) are cornered

'I couldn't stop. I swerved to the right,
I'll never forget the sound that night,
The cryin' tires, the bustin' glass,
The painful scream that I heard last.'
Death meant never having to grow up, never having to accept adult realities and values.

There was, of course, a lighter side to romance. In *Summer Love* (1958), starring Jill St John and Rod McKuen, the Daley Combo make a guest appearance at a summer camp with their hit song 'To Know You Is to Love You'. The same formula also lingered on in similar blends of rock and romance like *Juvenile Jungle* and *Let's Rock* (both 1958).

Eventually television supplied the movies with fresh teenage idols: Ed 'Kookie' Byrnes appeared in Sam Katzman's dreadful *Life Begins at 17* (1958). Cliff Richard was the British hipster in *Expresso Bongo* and the music business continued to supply stars for films like *Go Johnny Go* (both 1959) which starred Richie Valens, Eddie Cochran, The Cadillacs, The Flamingoes and Chuck Berry. The appearance, in 1959, of *Gidget* announced the arrival of the 'teen queen' – Sandra Dee.

By the end of the decade, serious considerations of teenage problems gave way to a tidal wave of beach and beat movies. *College Confidential* (dir. Albert S. Zugsmith, 1960) presented Mamie Van Doren as 'the student body', only this time the

by the police; most of them flee, but a few walk rebelliously into the glare of the squad cars' headlights. The mood of the scene perfectly matches the mean and moody spirit of the Shangri-Las' hit singles like 'Leader of the Pack'.

Similarly aggressive in tone were AIP's *Dragstrip Girl* and *Motorcycle Gang* (both 1957) which both featured the teen–parent conflicts, heroines torn between bad boyfriends and good boyfriends, plenty of hep jargon and high-speed motorbiking.

Katzman did not rule the teenage movie market alone: with *High School Confidential* (1958), Albert S. Zugsmith whipped up his own brand of hysteria. The film was notable for the introduction of the dope issue and the teenage star Mamie Van Doren. Zugsmith coined some 'jive talk' especially for the occasion and added plenty of scenes with hot-rod automobiles just for good measure. Soon 'reefer madness' became a hot theme in movies. In *The Cool and the Crazy* (1958) a kid who has served time in a state institution sells some dope to his classmates and even kills 'Eddie the Pusher' before himself succumbing and dying in a flaming car wreck in the middle of the desert.

Tragedies were becoming the very stuff of the teenage movie. AIP's *Dragstrip Riot* (1959) culminated in a free-for-all between two warring gangs of fast-living youths. In the record charts, the hit song 'Tom Dooley' (by the Kingston Trio) raised the morbid death song to a teenage art form but the phenomenon was to be attacked by the clergy and parent-teacher groups as depraved and corrupt. The first morbid death songs dealt with the demise of actual contemporary heroes like Johnny Ace and Buddy Holly. Truly great 'death discs' managed to pack all the trauma of teenage life into one metaphor – the big break-up. The songs had titles like 'Endless Sleep' and 'Teen Angel' and they were consciously up-to-date. Death came as a result of a stock-car race, or a rash dip in the river, or a joy ride in a borrowed car.

The victims always perished unexpectedly, accidentally and innocently. But, like their counterparts in the movies, they often made rash decisions. In 'Leader of the Pack' one falls in love with a boy whose love is more solid than his moped; 'I Want My Baby Back' proves how all the teenage casualties suffer horribly:

emphasis was equally on her professor, the well-known comedian Steve Allen. *Date Bait* (1960), a cheap and colourful 'exploitation' movie gave filmgoers a 'good' young couple who want to marry but get no help from their folks or her dope-crazy ex-boyfriend.

The trend towards wholesomeness continued with *Because They're Young* (1960), where the TV actor Dick Clark plays an ex-football star turned teacher, battling with youth problems in a high school in the style of *The Blackboard Jungle*. Finally, a film like *Where the Boys Are* (1959) demonstrates where the Fifties teenager had ended up. He or she was no longer a threat to civilized life, however many hi-jinks they might perpetrate. At the beginning of the Sixties, the movies saw the teenager as an energetic creature in need of advice and guidance, but meaning no real harm to society.

CYNTHIA ROSE

Above left: even the British promotion for the 'exploitation' double bill of Motorcycle Gang *and* Reform School Girl *(1957) pulled no punches, proving that sex and violence made movies marketable to teenage filmgoers too. Top: Ray Danton and Mamie Van Doren in* The Beat Generation *(1959). Above: Elvis Presley in the stylish but traditionally choreographed title number of* Jailhouse Rock *(1957), an early example of the tendency to cast rock'n'roll stars as maltreated and misunderstood*

'SAME PROBLEMS'- DIFFERENT PLACES'

The Fifties was the time when it seemed that the kids could do nothing right. A widening generation gap led society's older members to ask themselves what they should do with the young deliquents. One answer was – 'Film them!' They were different faces in different places – but the problems were the same

Above: Sal Mineo, Mark Rydell and John Cassavetes in Crime in the Streets *– Don Siegel's contribution to the popular study of gang warfare in violent urban settings*

Like all explosions, the youth explosion of the Fifties was messy. Never more so than when the delinquent fragments, flying outwards from too much coddling or manipulation, came home to roost in the flesh of the body politic. Society felt that it had never had it so bad from its juvenile members. As Peter Lewis wrote in his book *The Fifties*:

'The adult world first became aware of the process as a puzzling and disturbing increase in juvenile crime and delinquency. Crimes by offenders under twenty-one in England rose from 24,000 in 1955 to 45,000 in 1959.'

And this social malaise was world-wide. Movies echoed the statistics – either riding on the bandwagon of unease caused by the facts, or using the situation to say something beyond the immediate impact of the violent occasion. National characteristics were revealed in the way the idea was tackled.

Don Siegel's *Crime in the Streets* (1956) had precedents stretching back to William Wyler's *Dead End* (1937). While purporting to deal in almost stark documentary fashion with the problem of urban disintegration among the young, it manages to streak with sentimentality the characters inhabiting its decayed landscape.

Written by Reginald Rose, *Crime in the Streets* tells of Frankie, 18-year-old leader of a gang, and very much at large in the streets. Sal Mineo, a necessary actor-prop to support so many Hollywood movies with this theme, played another of the gang.

Menacing a man in those streets, Frankie finds his face slapped as though he were a child, and the bulk of the film is concerned with the ways in which he and his gang plot to kill the man for such an affront.

A scowling John Cassavetes as Frankie managed, often quite subtly, to create a character for whom there really should have been no redemption, no matter how much the friendly, neighbourhood social worker (James

Whitmore) professed to believe in him. That a kind of redemption comes – just as the knife is at the victim's throat – now seems at once arbitrary and contrived. It is in the grand old tradition of having your vicarious criminality and then renouncing it for righteousness' sake.

Siegel, who went on to make action thrillers that were far less ambivalent in their implications, is quoted in a BFI monograph by Alan Lovell:

'What was really wrong with the film was that it had a chilling identification for the average citizen who loathed the film. I think because there was no excuse for what these kids did. You know people identified themselves with the man who was beaten up.'

This was, of course, inevitable. The older members of the community watched with some apprehension the street-corner clusters of young people, using a convenient lamp-post as a base for their own aspiring community. But Frankie's alienation from the more mature world was an inner severance, which seemed to have little to do with the physical facts of the

only in Japan where it had great success perhaps because of the large number of gi[?] students who flocked to see it. But, in genera[?] other societies seemed scarcely to know wh[?] to do with their recalcitrant members – eve[?] when the delinquency was far from physica[?]

The layabouts in Fellini's *I Vitelloni* (195[?] *The Spivs*), for instance, are really just drifter[?] in a small Italian seaside town: older than mo[?] rebels of the time, although pregnancy is aga[?] a hinge for the story – a means of growing u[?] or growing away.

In this case Fausto (Franco Fabrizi), th[?] leader of the gang, is a Casanova who is force[?] to marry when his girl-friend Sandra (Leonor[?] Ruffo) expects a child. He continues his dis[?] solute ways until her departure makes hir[?] realize he has to settle down. A solution? N[?] really, because Sandra's brother has been s[?] disturbed by events that he decides to leav[?] home and town, to light out 'for where th[?] action is'. The rootless process continues, an[?] what might so easily have been a quite ban[?] story becomes, in Fellini's hands, a remarkabl[?] argument in his bleak assessment of huma[?] non-communication.

Les Quatre Cents Coups (1959, *The 400 Blow*[?] gives an insider's view of delinquency. Filtere[?] through his humanely poetic insight, it is th[?] 27-year-old François Truffaut's account of hi[?] own experiences at French reform school. Th[?] central character, Antoine Doinel (Jean-Pierr[?] Léaud) was to grow along with the directo[?] and the actor, who himself went on to mak[?] other movies about Doinel.

The first film, though, was especiall[?] moving because it showed Doinel as a 12-year[?]

established city within which he was contained.

The delinquents in the Polish *Piatka z Ulicy Barskiej* (1953, *Five Boys From Barska Street*), however, had no order against which to rebel, or at any rate it was an order being refurbished. They were already living among ruins – those of Warsaw in the period just following the Second World War. True, those shattered buildings were being rebuilt, but what to do about the quintet of young toughs around whom the film revolves? In true socialist manner, with an optimism that is as naive as it is adventurous, they are put to work on building a highway.

Director Aleksander Ford's narrative begins with the five placed on probation after being arrested for robbery with violence. Through their probation officer, who is also a bricklayer, they get jobs on the enormous East-West throughway. Most of the boys work in different ways on this project, although one finds work as a junior journalist; for another there is no hope. He has, it seems, 'strong Western allegiances' which make him want to blow up that symbolic link between East and West.

This crudity of approach is somewhat lessened by an understanding of the inarticulacy of such youths, even when talking among themselves. But the vicious gang leader is overdrawn and overheated as a Western-type thug determined to destroy solidarity. The optimism about the reclamation of all the boys (excluding the 'Westerner') therefore seems just as dubious; an evangelical tract for a political way of life.

The ritualistic Japanese life-style was just as much threatened by its young as any Western society, and a post-atomic reflection occurs in the *taiyozoku* films. One of the most persistently memorable of these is Kon Ichikawa's *Shokei No Heya* (1956, *Punishment Room*).

As Joseph I. Anderson and Donald Richie wrote in *The Japanese Film*:

'The concept of the *taiyozoku* (literally "sun tribe") is usually credited to the writer Shintaro Ishihara . . . and at the end of the novel there is a scene where the boy, at the funeral of the girl whom he made pregnant, cries out "You people don't understand anything." And it was this theme which was soon taken up by young people whose anarchistic ideas allowed them to think themselves members of the *taiyozoku*.'

At first much concerned with incidentals of rigid Japanese behaviour, the story gradually resolves itself into a consideration of those who would overthrow that order. A boy student

Above: Tadeusz Łomnicki and Tadeusz Janczar in a publicity still from the Polish film Five Boys From Barska Street, which looks at the incorrigible 'Western' attitudes of a young labourer. Below: Punishment Room shows that the Japanese were as concerned about delinquency as any other society. After raping a girl student (top), the boy rejects her and faces vicious retribution (bottom)

puts sleeping pills into the beer of a girl student, rapes her, and – when she later falls in love with him – spurns her for reasons best known to his own sense of spiritual order. The result is that he is badly beaten up.

Such real eye-for-an-eye punishment was doubtless gratifying to older audiences, not

...ld searching for love from his parents and ...chool, turning to stealing and disaffection, in ...he greedy hope that someone would see him ...s himself through his attention-getting de-...ices. But he does not even find hate in the ...eform school, where he is slapped with no ...egree of sadism, but rather as though it were ... mere routine.

It is a movie that ends with that famous ...reeze frame. Doinel runs to the sea shore and ...urns to look at us, crystallized suddenly into ...n enormous and painful question: what are ...ou going to do about me? It threw itself ...ompletely upon our mercy.

The greatest of all delinquency films showed ...o mercy at all. This was the Mexican *Los* ...*Olvidados* (1950), which was precariously ...alled *The Young and the Damned* by its Amer-...can distributors, but not by its Spanish direc-...or Luis Buñuel. When it won the Grand Prix ...or Direction and the International Critics' ...rize at the Cannes Film Festival in 1951, it ...arked Buñuel's return to film-making after a ...eriod in the wilderness.

He has called it a social film, but it is one of ...he few of its genre to transcend those limit-...tions of intent – it is not exploiting what it ...ees in order to make some glib comment. ...uñuel is merciless and direct in his treatment ...f the young gangsters observed in Mexico ...ity. They bully a blind man, take a legless ...ripple off the trolley on which he propels ...imself. Jaibo (Roberto Cobo), the vicious ...ader of the gang, is at once the director's ...onception of the 'free man' – but one who is ...hackled by his own urges.

He is hero-worshipped by the younger Pedro ...Alfonso Mejia), whose mother (Estela Inda) ...eeps with Jaibo. Sent to an outdoor farm-...eformatory, Pedro is trusted by the governor, ...ut – out on an errand – again comes under ...he violence of Jaibo. Both boys are killed.

Buñuel not only infiltrated his own specta-...ular brand of Surrealism into the film – ...otably a mother-loving dream sequence – but ...mposed on the whole a ruthless logic which ...recluded sentimentality. The kindly governor ...ho sends Pedro on an errand is typical of the ...ishy-washy liberalism which Buñuel, the ...narchist, despised. Liberal kindness leads to ...edro's death. And the blind man for whom we ...el initial sympathy is eventually shown to be ... cruel as his environment. About all the

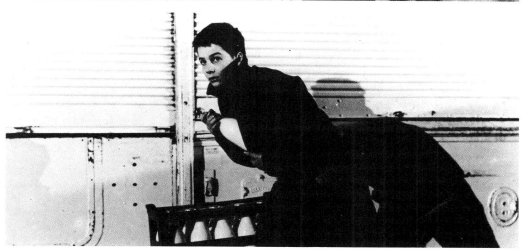

young, he screams: 'Tomorrow, tomorrow, we'll be finished with the lot of you!'

The muddled idealism of *Crime in the Streets* is a far cry from *Los Olvidados*. But chronologi-cally *Los Olvidados* comes first, showing how an artist can define and transmute a genre into his own aesthetic statement. He can also disquietingly answer his own questions about the causes of disorder.

The film ends with the body of Pedro being taken and thrown on the city dump: 'The body rolls over and over and we follow it down as it finally comes to rest.' In that shot is an indictment, not of the delinquents, but of the city – the rubbish from which they emerge and

Top: Fausto (Franco Fabrizi) and Sandra (Leonora Ruffo) with their love-child in Fellini's I Vitelloni. *Above: Jean-Pierre Léaud as Antoine Doinel in* Les Quatre Cents Coups *– the first of Truffaut's semi-autobiographical films with Doinel. Below left and right: scenes of cruelty and poverty from* Los Olvidados

to which they return. Society itself is seen as its own worst delinquent, a deity eating its off-spring, those young people struggling against its grasp before being devoured. It is still a vision of the condition that is the most comprehen-sively disturbing of the whole cycle.

TOM HUTCHINSON

James Dean was killed in a car crash on a Californian highway in the late afternoon of September 30, 1955, a fact that warranted little attention at the time. But within a couple of weeks, following the release of Dean's second major film, *Rebel Without a Cause*, he had become an idol for every *angst*-ridden teenager in America – and to this day remains the ultimate symbol of adolescent pain and rebellion born of despair

James Dean

Films sometimes speak with an intimacy that makes us forget everything but the people on screen. However inspired the construction, photographed presence is the viewer's dream, so urgent and personal that involuntary cries or movements may overtake us in the dark. It is as if the ghost up there had made love to us, *us* alone, in an act of divining, penetrating kindness. And if the ghost looks out into the darkness with the guarded knowingness of James Dean, then our being ravished is a ceremony in which reality and fiction are blurred by the enigma of a star's existence. The greatest stars know that nothing can make them as memorable as heartfelt hesitation. It is a way of commanding the threshold of the screen, not just working in the film like an actor.

People still think of him as vulnerable, but James Dean was the most dominating movie star since Garbo. Of course, Valentino's funeral and death cult were greater than Dean's, but 25 years after the silent star's death, his acting style had been eclipsed by Brando, Clift and Garfield. Dean died over 25 years ago, yet his style prevails, albeit with softer, less deadly exponents. No young actor today is as sinister as Dean was. No-one has his stealth, or seems as capable of redirecting a picture by virtue of sheer presence.

Rather than subscribe to the old myth that a

movie was a story being told, Dean knew that it was a fantasy that had to be lodged in the soul of the audience. Story was less relevant than the chance that imagery might fulfil emotional hope. Dean could speak, weep or cry out, to be sure, but he was most himself as a watchful, waiting actor. And because the films waited for him, the delay suggested a magical knowledge in Dean that was sensitive but frightening.

Like Garbo, he had a pessimistic vision of the world, and no amount of company could ease it. Indeed, cheerful groups and getting on well with life were the fabrications that most amused him. When he came to Hollywood for *East of Eden* (dir. Elia Kazan, 1955), Dean broke through all the bland hype of studio releases with this bleak admission of masquerade:

'A neurotic person has the necessity to express himself and my neuroticism manifests itself in the dramatic. Why do most actors act? To express the fantasies in which they have involved themselves.'

It is possible to measure Dean's brief glory, and the slow bruise of his legend, sociologically. He came along between the Beats and rock'n'roll. The generation that would slouch in his path included not just Paul Newman, Dennis Hopper and Steve McQueen, but Elvis, Dylan and every rock star. Dean found the clothes and gestures of young performance;

Above left: 'the resentful hair, the deep eyes floating in lonesomeness, the bitter beat look, the scorn on the lip' – words from a poem by John Dos Passos that admirably capture the James Dean image. Below: Dean as the glowering Cal Trask with Julie Harris and Raymond Massey in East of Eden

the grace of loneliness

nam, network TV, assassinations, plastic ecology and American self-doubt. *Rebel* was not simply a film about high school: after all, the age of the actors was closer to 24. The picture had more to do with its director Nicholas Ray's pioneering discontent with America – as vivid, rueful and self-destructive as the director himself, who had found an actor so attuned to that atmosphere that Ray must have marvelled at the lucid enactment of his own anguish:

'The conflict between giving himself and fear of giving in to his own feelings . . . a vulnerability so deeply embedded that one is instantly moved, almost disturbed by it. Since infancy he had engaged in this struggle between impulsive violence and a grand defiance.'

That is Ray talking about the actor, but actually identifying himself, and indicating that the director who would do no major work for the last 16 years of his life, but wandered in a haze of outcast vitality and brooding self-pity, was yet another whose life was affected by James Dean. And Ray was possibly more vulnerable than Dean, who never bothered to conceal a furtive alienation from others, a kind of calculation that indicated a future career as a director and a producer.

Dean's life had the requisite elements of tragedy that biographers would pick over. But we cannot know if he was ever as disturbed as they would be. He was born in Indiana in 1931 and moved to Los Angeles as a young child. His mother died there when he was nine. Dean went back to the farmlands of Indiana to live with an aunt and uncle, during which time he saw little of his father. After ten years he

hots from Robert Altman's documentary The ames Dean Story *(1957): Dean on 52nd treet while staying in New York (above); mmy, age nine, shortly after going to live ith his aunt and uncle (top right); in the entre of the front row of the Fairmount High chool baseball team (below right)*

but, before that, he authorized the acting out of teenage problems. He marks the very first self-conscious younger generation. This was not just the potency of a new audience, but the commercialization of lonely hostility to the establishment. Dean negotiated the transition from Andy Hardy growing into his allotted place in the American Dream, to rock's intransigence, surly hipsterism and the wholesale denial of American values.

When Warners advertised *Rebel Without a Cause* (1955), they believed they had been lucky enough to catch the slipstream of a phenomenon known as juvenile delinquency. But Dean's radicalism was an existential disenchantment anticipating the squalor of Viet-

Right: Dean as Jett Rink, an embittered outcast who strikes oil on the land that formerly belonged to his employers, the Benedicts, in Giant. *Below: as Jim Stark, taunted by his schoolmates in* Rebel Without a Cause – *a stranger even among his own kind*

returned to California in search of an acting school. That was in 1949, in six years Dean would be dead. His work was so lyrical that there is no plausible way of tracing it to unhappiness. The legend quickly smothered facts. It alleged he was morose *and* appealing, that he searched for a mother substitute, loved the sweet Pier Angeli, slept with anyone available, was drawn to homosexual encounters, practised self-abuse, and so on and so on until the wreckage of a Porsche Spyder embodied the tangle of possibilities.

As if to solve his own confusion, he was determined to be an actor. Acting, and the moments of lying, are the only times our minds are set. Every character he played on screen is brimming with that pretence. They are all dreamers, hiding behind shifty materialists. It is as if he knew there was a darkness somewhere, as awesome as the planetarium in *Rebel*, and that if he looked into it, then he would be resolved, happy and unhappy, evil and benign, seeing and being seen. He wanted us, like a ghost in search of a house to haunt.

With scant training he had made a name for himself on Broadway and in live television drama. In 1954 he won a Tony Award as the Arab boy in *The Immoralist*, a play adapted from Gide's novel. On television, he had so entranced directors with his improvisations that the irritation of such co-stars as Mary Astor and Paul Lukas was overruled and they were told to let Jimmy do it his way. They were prototype parent figures, rebuked by his insight and required to stand to attention while his muse climbed. Dean was a jazz actor who could solo at will from the set chords, never repeating himself. He could reduce Raymond Massey, Natalie Wood or Elizabeth Taylor to rhythm sections anxious to support the rapture with which he occupied the moment. It is acting that dares boredom and breakdown and threatens such things as text and production with perilous delays, new lines and inspirational bits of business. It came just before

cinéma-vérité, and it makes all that actuality look banal and hollow. Dean had stylized the real more than anyone before or since.

It got him into trouble on the stage and it impeded his last film, *Giant* (1956). But he was lucky to have Nicholas Ray and Elia Kazan as his first directors, because they both needed him and were both lifted by the occasion. Kazan had exactly the training and disposition

to understand Dean's sulky method. More important, Dean's improvisation freed the pent-up but often schematic emotionalism in Kazan. The film of *East of Eden* is a staggering glorification of the immature distress of adolescence. Kazan dropped 90 per cent of the Steinbeck novel and refashioned the last part as his own psycho-drama. He made it the mirror of a personal rebellion against his own father. The fantasy revealed on the screen that of parenthood brought down to the level of adolescent wishful recrimination. In terms of box-office history, *East of Eden* is the first teenage weepie, never questioning the central figure's tantrum at being neglected or misunderstood. Cal Trask is a tyrant of feelings, an *enfant terrible* actor in a household of characters, demanding a father's love, aiming to buy it and confronting an envied stooge brother with their mother's shocking existence. Cal may not be Cain, but he has a taste for self-serving melodrama that rivals Citizen Kane's. But because of Kazan's complicity, so Dean's performance confounds reason or maturity. In its form, *East of Eden* is one of the most uncompromisingly romantic American films. In letting the teenage yearning soar uncorrected, it becomes a testament to vibrant infantilism, with the hero and the heroine left to play house and the father reduced to the status of a doll.

Dean is supposedly playing a 20-year-old but Cal could be as old as Dracula. Vampirism is explicit in extreme stardom – and it is spelled

ut in the action of Kazan's film as every other
haracter succumbs to Cal's view of the world.
ean preys upon the others and upon the
udience. As the camera indulges his pauses,
o it flatters his authority. *East of Eden* is a
isconcertingly languid film because Kazan
as relinquished his own decisiveness to
ean's rhapsody upon hurt feelings. Cinema-
cope seemed hallowed because it allowed
nore space for Dean's nervy prowling.

Rebel did the same, from Dean's foetal pose
efore the credits to his spread-eagled agony as
e tells the police he had removed the bullets
rom Plato's gun. Ray's film seemed con-
emporary, but Dean crooned Wagner in the
recinct station and surveyed Natalie Wood
ke a dissipated Hamlet contemplating a drug-
tore Ophelia. Dean seems so much more
ware than parents, police, teachers or other
ids. He could be a traveller from the past or
rom one of those remote planets he watches in
ne ominous theatre of space. He knows a level
f feeling that this Californian society is numb
o, and it confers on him the pain and privilege
f a poet, or a director.

Jim Backus, the actor who played Dean's
ather in *Rebel*, told *Variety*, 'This is the first
me in the history of motion pictures that a 24-
ear-old boy, with only one movie to his credit,
ras practically the co-director.' Years after
iant, director George Stevens regretted that
e had not given Dean more license. In
articular, there is a scene where Jett Rink
omes to a party at the Reata ranch and
ccepts a drink. Dean wanted Jett to use his
wn flask so that he would be beholden to none. Such a ploy was characteristic of Dean,
oo: he wanted to usurp his directors, and he
ad his eyes set on making his own films.

But on *Giant*, a solemn and respectable
irector could only see that the solid Texan
umily was better behaved than the oil-trash
id who becomes a tycoon. Whenever Dean

*Above: Dean with Nicholas Ray: they planned
to work together again after discovering great
creative rapport while making* Rebel Without a
Cause. *Below: 'Racing is the only time I feel
whole' – James Dean in his first Porsche at a
race meeting early in 1955, and with destiny
in his hands*

has a scene on his own – pacing his land or
splashing in the oil – his ability to reach us
physically, and to idealize solitude, bring the
film to life. He makes a more committed effort
to ageing than either Rock Hudson or Elizabeth Taylor, and his performance lets us see
something not appreciated by Stevens: that the
nobody who becomes a lord of Texas is more
interesting and just as American as the self-
satisfied Benedicts.

When Dean died, François Truffaut recog-
nized that his acting had not been psychological or focused on the text. It was a delicate
escape, set in the manner of naturalism, from
raw being into a butterfly performance. It
seems to be made up on the spur of his moment
and our dream. That immediacy was what
enlisted us in the transformation. For it was an
assertion of make-believe such as we must
make whenever we watch a movie personage
at once so real and so phantom. Truffaut
compared Dean with Chaplin – there was the
same facade of downcast failure turning into
glittering control and perfection:

'Something else is at work, a poetic game
that lends authority to every liberty – even
encourages it. Acting right or wrong has no
meaning when we talk about Dean, because
we expect a surprise a minute from
him . . . With James Dean everything is grace,
in every sense of the word . . . He isn't better
than everybody else; he does *something else*, the
opposite; he protects his glamour from the
beginning to the end of each film.'

DAVID THOMSON

Filmography
1951 Fixed Bayonets; Sailor Beware. **'52** Has
Anybody Seen My Gal? **'55** East of Eden; Rebel
Without a Cause. **'56** Giant.

JAMES DEAN
NATALIE WOOD
SAL MINEO

In Warner Bros.

"REBEL WITHOUT A CAUSE"

CINEMASCOPE
AND WARNERCOLOR

...and they both come from 'good' families!

Directed by Nicholas Ray, 1955
Prod co: Warner Bros. **prod:** David Weisbart. **sc:** Stewart Stern, Irving Shulman, from a story by Nicholas Ray. **photo:** Ernest Haller. **ed:** William Zeigler. **art dir:** Malcolm Bart. **mus dir:** Leonard Rosenman. **r/t:** 111 minutes.
Cast: James Dean (*Jim*), Natalie Wood (*Judy*), Jim Backus (*Jim's father*), Ann Doran (*Jim's mother*), Rochelle Hudson (*Judy's mother*), William Hopper (*Judy's father*), Sal Mineo (*Plato*), Corey Allen (*Buzz*), Dennis Hopper (*Goon*), Edward Platt (*Ray*), Steffi Sidney (*Mil*), Marietta Canty (*maid*), Ian Wolfe (*lecturer*), Frank Mazzola (*Crunch*).

Ray's Rebel Without a Cause is one of those films that provokes a violent reaction – even in those who have never seen it. When it was premiered in Britain, it was greeted with moral outrage. *The Spectator* said:

'Its solemnity is rather irritating, seeing that a few good spanks would settle a lot of its problems.'

The *Daily Sketch* critic praised Nicholas Ray's direction but warned: 'That kind of brilliance in this kind of picture can be dangerous.'

Rebel Without a Cause is, of course, a 'problem picture' in the honourable Warner's tradition and can trace its ancestry back through the Dead End Kids' movies and *Angels With Dirty Faces* (1938) to the founding principles of 'social conscience' drama. In the wake of location-shot thrillers like *Gun Crazy* (1949) and alongside con-

temporary 'teenpix' – B movies like *Five Against the House* (1955) – *Rebel Without a Cause* looks even more like the 'realist' romance it is. But Nicholas Ray and screenwriter Stewart Stern made determined efforts to accommodate a documentary feel within the parameters of the high-gloss, A-feature production values required at Warners.

Ray and Stern spent weeks interviewing youth leaders and court officers. They sat in on juvenile court sessions and spoke with criminologists including one who had been the chief psychiatrist at the Nuremberg trials. They did their homework.

The scenario, as Eric Rohmer observed in the French magazine of film theory *Cahiers du Cinéma* in 1955, falls neatly into the five acts of classical tragedy: exposition, with the conflict between the parents

and the children clearly stated; act two, in which Jim befriends Plato and is taunted by Buzz; act three, which includes the 'chicken run' with its fatal climax; act four, where Jim and Judy enjoy a transitory peace and share their love with Plato; and the final tragic act whose full impact is engraved on Jim's anguished face. As befits Aristotle's rules, the action is all but contained within 24 hours.

With that kind of narrative compression, the film could have emerged as hysterical melodrama, but even in the emotionally climactic scene of the domestic quarrel, the audience is never allowed to assume a dispassionate, 'objective' perspective. 'We are all involved!' as Jim exclaims. Ray's direction is in control: his camera spins upright out of a brilliant inverted shot from Jim's viewpoint. He then forces the action of the argument across the room and back against the stairs for greater dramatic effect and intercuts low-angle, high-angle and obliquely distorted shots to disrupt the perspective that the viewer normally considers his or her privilege. It is a bravura piece of direction in a film whose *mise-en-scène* is elsewhere distinguished by set-pieces, like the 'chicken run' and the final planetarium scenes – both of which are staged under the artificial, theatrical lighting of a circle of car headlamps.

The real director of *Rebel Without a Cause*, however, may be James Dean, in the sense that the film critic David Thomson describes him 'redirecting the picture by virtue of sheer presence'. If the complex experience of reading a film can be premised on the *look* constantly exchanged between the

viewer and the on-screen protagonists, then *direction* may be construed as the control and orientation of that look. The unique qualities of James Dean as an actor, especially in the intuitive relationship he shared with Nicholas Ray, permit the 'lingering' of the look (Dean's characteristic pauses) and provoke the disorientation of the look (his restlessness in the CinemaScope frame). In short, Dean tells us where to look and what to notice.

In the scene where Jim meets Judy outside her house at night, we anticipate the confirmation of the love between them and, therefore, might expect a progression from individual close-ups, to two-shot, to embrace. Instead, shooting in medium close-up, Ray shows Jim, agitated, lolling or rolling over, dominating the central and left areas of the vast CinemaScope image, while Judy remains almost motionless right of frame. The framing, like everything else in the film, privileges Dean, confirming his dominance and suggesting that Ray was taking advantage of this opportunity to play Dean as his *alter ego* and extend the art of directing through performance so that Dean can be seen as acting out Ray's romantic fantasy. To quote David Thomson again:

'Arguably only Nicholas Ray could have given Dean a part that guessed at the looming alienation in America.'

Dean and Ray were two loners from Middle America, down there in the comfortable (studio-set) suburban homes, who fled to the wide-open spaces of a mansion in the hills and an observatory that showed moving pictures of the heavens.   MARTYN AUTY

Jim, the adolescent son of middle-class parents recently moved to California, is run in for drunkeness by the police (1). He sobers up and has a sympathetic hearing from the juvenile-offenders officer (2).

The following day, Jim's first day at his new high school, he meets Judy and her gang of rowdy friends. In the course of a school visit to the local planetarium, Jim becomes friendly with Plato, an unbalanced, orphaned kid seeking affection. Outside the planetarium Jim is taunted into a fight with Buzz (3), the leader of the pack and Judy's boyfriend. They agree to meet later that evening for a 'chicken run' – an endurance test in which each will drive an old car to the cliff edge and leap clear at the last possible moment.

Seeking, but failing to get, advice from his father, Jim joins Buzz at the rendezvous (4). They line up (5), Judy signals the start of the race and the cars head for the cliff-edge. Buzz's sleeve catches in the doorhandle causing him to go over the edge with the car. Jim consoles Judy and drives her home.

Jim feels he must go to the police but his parents object: a violent quarrel ensues (6). However, Jim goes to the police station and is seen by Buzz's gang-mates (7). They swear to get even with him.

Picking up Judy on the way, Jim drives to a large deserted house in the hills where they are joined by Plato (8). Jim and Judy declare their love (9). Buzz's gang follow them there and beat up Plato who nevertheless manages to shoot one of them. The police arrive and chase Plato to the planetarium.

Jim finally persuades the frightened Plato to give himself up but, at the crucial moment, shots are fired from the police cordon and Plato falls down. An anguished Jim zips up the jacket on his friend's body and escorts Judy from the scene.

Right: setting up the final scene in which Plato is lured from the planetarium to his death

HIGH-SCHOOL YEARS

High schools. Seats of learning or hot-beds of trouble? Apples for the teacher or flick-knives in the locker-room? The new teenage subculture was ripe for exploitation, but was Hollywood willing to condone rebellion?

Top left: Russ Tamblyn, Jan Sterling and Mamie Van Doren as student, teacher and sexy aunt in High School Confidential. *Bottom left Brandon de Wilde and Carol Lynley in* Blue Denim. *Above: A* Summer Place *starred teen idols Troy Donahue and Sandra Dee*

After Nicholas Ray's 1955 masterpiece, *Rebel Without a Cause*, there really was no need for more movies about high-school punks. Ray and his star James Dean had defined the emergent teenage subculture perfectly, even dignifying it philosophically – which is one thing that places the movie a cut above Marlon Brando's alternative archetype in *The Wild One* two years earlier. *Rebel Without a Cause* did not discover anything – there had been movies about smart, wild kids torn between innocence and experience since the Thirties – but it did put a new, suburban face on the situation. That was why it was frightening and exhilarating, the movie could have been set anywhere, Dean's Jim Stark could have been any kid.

Unfortunately, *Rebel Without a Cause* also established the existence of a new market ripe for exploitation, and in the mid-Fifties – with Hollywood just coming off the ropes after its initial confrontation with television – it could not afford to pass up any opportunities. Thus, the birth of a genre.

However, the movie had suggested that punk nihilism and pointless violence were appropriate social responses to post-Atom-Bomb existence, and Hollywood hardly had

the stomach for a series of films which went so far into sociology. Therefore, the teen films that followed, in the great liberal tradition of hedged bets, traced the lives of virtue rewarded despite all the evidence and served more to salve the consciences of the adults in the audience – 'They really want to be normal, Pop' – than to convince wayward youth of the futility of carving up seats in the balconies.

But adults were not in the audience for the most part. As a consequence, the punks in the cheap seats took delight in subverting the themes of movies like *The Blackboard Jungle* (1955), *High School Confidential* (1958) – meant to be a typical high-school movie but which overdid the 'James Dean' role – *A Summer Place* (1959) and, in the same year, *Blue Denim* – in which a 'nice' boy gets a 'nice' girl pregnant. Did the director Richard Brooks really expect teenagers to identify with Glenn Ford's fuddy-duddy teacher or Sidney Poitier's defeated before-he-starts student in *The Blackboard Jungle*? Hardly likely with a comic-villainous character such as Vic Morrow's Artie to serve as thrilling counterpoint.

Poitier's hang-dog student is supposed to be redeemed by the sweet pieties of Dadier (Glenn Ford) but he looks as beaten at the end of the

movie – a good kid still trapped in dead-en surroundings – as he did at the beginning Whatever success he has found is at best dul and the point of *Rebel Without a Cause* was tha kids were willing to sacrifice anything, eve respectability, to break through boredom.

Therefore what we remember from *Th Blackboard Jungle* are the credits with B Haley's insistent, rumbling 'One, two, thre o'clock, four o'clock, Rock!' and the anarchi breakthroughs of the hoodlum classmates the demolition of Dadier's collection of date jazz records, that grand moment when Arti (Vic Morrow), a true incorrigible, stands up i the classroom and flicks open his switchblad

It makes no difference that Greg (Poitier) wi stomp Artie all over the classroom (imagin the chances of that really happening in ghetto school). Artie has refused to succumb t the preachments of restraint and in that on moment, however sadistic, he has broke loose. He is the only free man on the screen Who would you rather grow up to be?

And so it goes through many sequels, few them so memorable, the punk rampant in th faces of Morrow, Sal Mineo, Russ Tamblyn an the other ferret-faced bad guys who are still th most exciting faces on the screen. If *The Black*

...ard Jungle is the most memorable of these ...ms, it is still only a half-step above the rest. Still, it at least has the advantage of a fairly ...thentic setting – some unspecified urban ...um – and its avoidance of sexuality. When ...e punk movie moved into the upper-class ...burbs of A Summer Place – about the love ...fair of a teenage couple and the parallel affair ...tween the girl's father and the boy's mother ...and its ilk, the kids became miniaturized ...ults with hardly anyone as interesting as ...orrow's Artie appearing, even briefly. And ...hen Hollywood tried to deal with a sexual ...orld in which teenage boys carried condoms ...their wallets as a pledge of allegiance, ...atters became genuinely hopeless.

What finally doomed the Fifties genre of ...enage movies was their treatment of adol...cent angst as a serious social problem. ...eryone, except the Hollywood producers ...d directors who made such tripe, under...ood that teenagers would outgrow their ...intless rebelliousness soon enough, in the ...tural course of things – which is another ...ason why such films are only as good as the ...carious hoodlum kicks they provide.

It took Gidget (1959) to make it obvious that ...en kids got the joke on themselves. Gidget ...ayed the teenage dilemma as farce, and while ...was hardly less unbelievable in its details, it ...ould spawn a series of beach-party movies ...hich took both the pain and the glory of ...ing a kid in this period for granted, and ...nbellished such situations with enough ...rills and sexuality to justify sitting through ...em with more than a sneer.

True enough, Gidget's plot is as thin and silly ...any of the punk problem pictures which ...eceded it, and its image of the disaffected ...uth is hardly less ludicrous: James Darren, ...the rebel surfer Moondoggie is purely a ...reppie'. But the movie makes Gidget's battle ...ith her virginity the joke that it is – most of ...e movie revolves around her working up ...urage to Do It, not philosophizing about why ...e should not. And Gidget at least begins to get ...e details of teenage culture right: the slang, ...e clothing, the cars, the surfing, the beach-

parties. All that is missing is the music. The movie even offers a sympathetic adult figure, Cliff Robertson's Kahoona, who dispenses surfing wisdom and is not undercut even by the final revelation that he is really an aircraft pilot turned alcoholic. Sandra Dee starred and immediately became an idol for 'ordinary' girls to imitate and young boys to desire.

But, Gidget's producers missed the point and the series petered out as Kennedy-era, Andy Hardy, clean, boring fun for grown-ups. But over at the maverick American International Pictures – which had done an even earlier farcical teen picture, I Was a Teenage Werewolf (1957) – the lesson was not lost.

By 1963 the beach-party movies were in full swing, followed by a series of hot-rod and motorcycle movies which took the burgeoning teen culture at face value. In the American International Pictures' beach and bike movies, detail was everything; if society's values are invariably restored by the final scene, the 90 minutes which precede it simply wink at the concept that there could be anything better than living young, fast and hard. The American International Pictures' movies also finally got the music together, primarily by imitating vocalists such as Frankie Avalon, Fabian and Annette, and then later by setting up original

Above: a showdown for teacher Glenn Ford in The Blackboard Jungle. *Below left: Kahoona (Cliff Robertson) and Moondoggie (James Darren) vie for the affections of* Gidget *(Sandra Dee). Below:* The Wild Angels *with Peter Fonda and Nancy Sinatra*

rock scores for such films as Roger Corman's The Wild Angels (1966).

Naturally, teen pictures remained trash even in their heyday; no major director or star was likely to risk credibility by getting involved with such low-budget exploitation, but out of the beach-party and biker movies came a new generation of Hollywood stars. Among them were actors like Jack Nicholson and Bruce Dern, and directors like John Boorman – whose Catch Us If You Can (1965) marked the debut of a distinguished career. Of course, it was the beach-party-to-motorcycle movie cycle which eventually led to Easy Rider (1969), which again opened the door to a new generation of movie-makers.

Despite it all, then, the teenage punk picture had its role to play in cinema history, as well as weathering Hollywood through the early television years. This is not much, but given its benighted beginnings, it probably qualifies as a happy ending anyhow.   DAVE MARSH

THE KINGS OF ROCK
ARE ROLLIN' BACK TO THE SCREEN...
IN THEIR
BIGGEST!

BILL HALEY AND HIS COMETS

Don't Knock The Rock

MADE BY THE PRODUCERS OF "ROCK AROUND THE CLOCK"!

CO-STARRING
ALAN DALE

ALAN FREED

THE TRENIERS

LITTLE RICHARD

DAVE APPELL AND HIS APPLEJACKS

with JOVADA and JIMMY BALLARD
Written by ROBERT E. KENT and JAMES B. GORDON · Produced by SAM KATZMAN
Directed by FRED F. SEARS · A CLOVER PRODUCTION · A COLUMBIA PICTURE

Left: on radio, Alan Freed spun a mean turntable on film, as in this star-studded movie, he became the ever-present man behind the microphone. Above: Rock, Pretty Baby highlighted a typical do-it-yourself 'garage' rock band which featured several well-known teen-stars

By the mid-Fifties teenagers had ceased to be 'a phenomenon' and had become 'an issue'. Sex and Drugs and Rock'n'Roll were in the news. But Youth Revolt was soon packaged as Youth Culture: moderated, sold short and sold back. Hollywood logic prevailed: why try to understand 'em when you can more profitably exploit 'em?

While the big studios, by and large, perpetuated the 'social-worker' syndrome of liberal concern and moral recuperation, the buck-hungry independents kept one eye on the Top 40 or the Hot 100 and proceeded to cram as many rock'n'roll stars as they could muster into cheapo quickies with infinitely serviceable formula plots and zero artistic pretensions. *Don't Knock the Rock* (1956), the sequel to producer Sam Katzman's ground-breaking *Rock Around the Clock* (also 1956), became the watchword for a whole series of teen-flicks designed to thrill the kids, while reassuring their frantic parents that junior would not turn

zomboid under the now-notorious rock'n'roll influence.

If Bill Haley's cutesy kiss-curl would not do that particular trick, there was usually the sober and mature presence of pioneering DJ and impresario Alan Freed as guarantor of the music's harmlessness. No hint here of impending 'payola' scandals; certainly no hint of sex and drugs; and even though director Frank Tashlin got in early in the cycle with his brilliant satire on the show-business hype of the 'new' phenomenon, *The Girl Can't Help It* (1956), it made little difference to the sickeningly wholesome image of celluloid rock.

Virtually chaperoned before the cameras by Alan Freed, in such frenzied nonsense as *Rock, Rock, Rock* (1956), *Mister Rock and Roll* (1957) and *Go, Johnny, Go* (1959), even the likes of Chuck Berry, Little Richard, Frankie Lymon and Eddie Cochran could look like exemplary heroes for upright American boys to emulate — 'they might *look* a little weird, but have you seen how much they earn?' And if the budget would not run to guest appearances by genuine rockers, imitation became the name of the game. The hopeful high-school combo became a staple feature of the genre, few could boast the incongruous line-up in *Rock, Pretty Baby* (1957) which included teen-stars Sal Mineo on drums, John Saxon on sax and Rod McKuen(!) on bass. The girls got a look-in too, with the precocious Tuesday Weld (15) playing 18, and dubbed by Connie Francis, leading the way in *Rock, Rock, Rock*. The problems of puppy-love, uptight parents an

the
Rock

Above right: Elvis Presley, suitably subdued for the movies, with his bevy of garlanded girls in Blue Hawaii (1961). Right: another of the three films in 1956 in which Alan Freed, the godfather of rock, appeared alongside a host of rock'n'roll stars

what to wear at the school Prom took up most of the energies of the non-musical teen-stars.

Too much sweetness and light could get a bit cloying though, so there were naturally a few low-budget delinquent entries to sour the teenage dream. In efforts like *Juvenile Jungle*, *Hot Car Girl* and *The Cool and the Crazy* (all 1958), a forgotten actor like Richard Bakalyan could rise to brief superstar status in the genre as an all-purpose corrupter/dope-pusher/gang leader, while genuine Fifties icon Mamie Van Doren was often on hand to emphasize the dangers of adolescent lust at the very moment she was provoking it. Ace producer Albert S. Zugsmith mastered the art of the teen-exposé with *High School Confidential* (1958), and offered *The Beat Generation* (1959) and *College Confidential* (1960) for dessert. Such movies, along with other luridly-titled teases like *Untamed Youth* (1957) and *Dragstrip Riot* (1959), rarely featured the image-conscious rock stars,

and often relegated the music itself to mere accompaniment.

Most blatantly image-conscious of the rockers was The King himself. Elvis Presley on television had been framed from the waist up to avoid any shots of the notoriously energetic pelvis. But Presley in the movies presented no such erotic threat – the pelvis never even twitched in *Love Me Tender* (1956) which symptomatically introduced Presley as a cine-matic balladeer. He even died on screen in two of his first four movies to stress his mainstream dramatic credentials. Of all his increasingly awful movies, only *Jailhouse Rock* (1957) conveys anything of the guts of rock'n'roll, while only *Flaming Star* (1960), as a Don Siegel film, still attracts cineastes.

Other rockers flirted with the mainstream as the musical genre became increasingly thread-bare, but even Ricky Nelson, who made it as

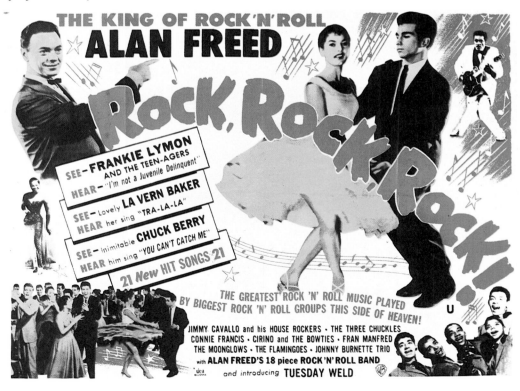

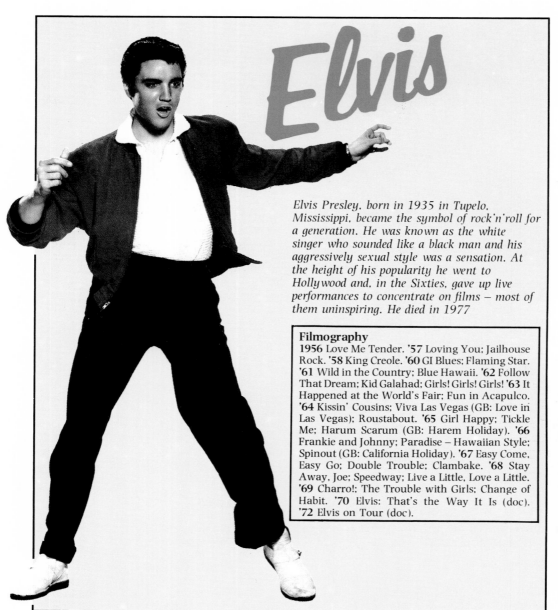

Elvis

Elvis Presley, born in 1935 in Tupelo, Mississippi, became the symbol of rock'n'roll for a generation. He was known as the white singer who sounded like a black man and his aggressively sexual style was a sensation. At the height of his popularity he went to Hollywood and, in the Sixties, gave up live performances to concentrate on films – most of them uninspiring. He died in 1977

Filmography
1956 Love Me Tender. '57 Loving You; Jailhouse Rock. '58 King Creole. '60 GI Blues; Flaming Star. '61 Wild in the Country; Blue Hawaii. '62 Follow That Dream; Kid Galahad; Girls! Girls! Girls! '63 It Happened at the World's Fair; Fun in Acapulco. '64 Kissin' Cousins; Viva Las Vegas (GB: Love in Las Vegas); Roustabout. '65 Girl Happy; Tickle Me; Harum Scarum (GB: Harem Holiday). '66 Frankie and Johnny; Paradise – Hawaiian Style; Spinout (GB: California Holiday). '67 Easy Come, Easy Go; Double Trouble; Clambake. '68 Stay Away, Joe; Speedway; Live a Little, Love a Little. '69 Charro!; The Trouble with Girls; Change of Habit. '70 Elvis: That's the Way It Is (doc). '72 Elvis on Tour (doc).

high as Howard Hawks' *Rio Bravo* (1959), failed to sustain a film-actor reputation.

Back on Poverty Row, the first wave of teen-movies was finally killed off by a sudden rush of beach movies. The chart success of Jan and Dean and the Beach Boys, plus the inexplicable popularity of Columbia's Gidget series, which had sun, sand and Sandra Dee, led American International Pictures and director William Asher to juggle Frankie Avalon and Annette Funicello, beach bunnies and beatniks, a square academic and a dumb biker into a morbidly fascinating comedy called *Beach Party* (1963). It sold, but its imitative successors were swamped by a new phenomenon: Beatlemania.

The rock movies of the late Fifties and early Sixties constitute little more than a footnote in cinema history, largely because Hollywood persisted in regarding the music and its pioneer practitioners as a passing commercial fad. It has been left to a new wave of young American film-makers to give the decade its retrospective due as the first golden age of rock. George Lucas started a nostalgia boom with *American Graffiti* (1973), featuring veteran DJ Wolfman Jack as spiritual father to the cruisin' generation. More recently, there has been a trend to reverently revisionist period-piece biopics. Steve Rash's *The Buddy Holly Story* (1978)

and John Carpenter's *Elvis* (1979) clearly proclaim their heroes, while Richard Compton's *Deadman's Curve* (1978) fêted Jan and Dean, and Floyd Mutrux's *American Hot Wax* (1978) brought it all full circle by immortalizing Mister Rock'n'roll himself, Alan Freed. The beat goes on . . .   PAUL TAYLOR

Top: The Beat Generation was given the hard sell by producer Albert S. Zugsmith. Above: Tuesday Weld, seen here in Rock, Rock, Rock, became a central figure in the teendream. Below: Alan Freed and the legend of rock'n'roll were finally paid their dues in the Seventies with American Hot Wax

Juke BoxJungle

he Beatles were on their way, the Rolling Stones were being born, nd British rock'n'roll was taking its first unsteady steps towards he cinemas. But this was the Fifties – good-clean-fun and all-round-ntertainment were just what the kids wanted

'hen rock'n'roll music started figuring in the anning schedules of film producers in the SA, it was already a key ingredient in the p-music world, having moulded its own sub-lture involving artists, fans and fashions. It as far from hitting any kind of excitement ak, but it was there.

Then, in 1955, the feature film *The Black-ard Jungle* appeared. It was a pretty raightforward classroom drama but it had a adline-making extra – Bill Haley and his mets playing 'Rock Around the Clock' over

the credits. To the near-worldwide sound of audiences' stomping feet and the slashing of seats, cinematic rock was on its way. Elvis Presley emerged next as rock's first solo super-star in a feature film which was to have been called *The Reno Brothers*, but became *Love Me Tender* (1956), the title of the main vocal theme.

This flurry of frenetic action, which in-cluded *The Girl Can't Help It* (1956), starring the pneumatic Jayne Mansfield and a host of Top 50 singers, as the first major colour film to feature rock, created wide interest in Britain.

Stage package shows, generally featuring near unknowns, rocked round Britain, and the record companies started cashing in. The British film industry finally woke up to the potential of rock on celluloid in 1957, but it took up the challenge with severe self-doubt, an obvious lack of know-how and a hit-or-miss philosophy.

Stainless Steele

Two of the earliest contenders for the title of Britain's Elvis were Tommy Steele and Frankie Vaughan – the first a one-time merchant seaman and the other a dead ringer for Victor Mature. Steele (b. 1936) – whose career was masterminded from coffee-bar singing to star-ring at the London Palladium by Larry Parnes, a refugee from the rag trade, and John Ken-nedy, a gimmick-conscious photographer – was initially a genuine rock superstar. Yet, strangely enough, he had comparatively few hit records, and by 1960 had turned his back on rock and become an early example of the all-round-entertainer syndrome.

Steele's rags-to-riches saga was celebrated in *The Tommy Steele Story* in 1957. It was originally planned as a documentary on Brit-ish rock'n'roll, but that was before the pro-ducers fell prey to the persuasive powers of the Parnes-Kennedy team; skiffle, calypso and traditional jazz were added. The toothy singer went on to films like *The Duke Wore Jeans* (1958) and *Tommy the Toreador* (1959), but it was soon apparent that his heart was not in trying to become a Presley-patterned performer.

Find-a-Presley

There were very real (but short-lived) hopes that Frankie Vaughan (b. 1928) would be Britain's home-grown rock superstar. He made his debut on screen in 1957 in *These Dangerous Years* – a song-studded story about law-defying Liverpool teenagers – co-starring with Carole Lesley. And for a while, in the British 'find-a-Presley' campaign, it seemed Terry Dene (b. 1938) might fill the bill. 'White Sport Coat' (original by Mary Robbins) was his only hit record, but his lower lip curled Elvis-like

Top: Serious Charge – Cliff plays it cool in a coffee bar, perfect venue for the juke-box beat. Below left: Joe Brown (on bar) in Three Hats for Lisa *(1965). Below: despite the 'sensation', Frankie Vaughan quickly took a back seat in the race to stardom*

Above: ageless Cliff Richard taking a hip Summer Holiday. *Above left:* Tommy the Toreador – *a bravura Spanish fantasy comes t[o] life for seaman Tommy. Left: another dual identity for Tommy Steele as the cockney doub[le] of a young Duke in* The Duke Wore Jeans. *Bottom left: Claire Gordon, Shirley Ann Field, Gillian Hills, Adam Faith in* 'Beat' Girl. *Only Faith continues to act rather than sing*

and he was good on stage. So Dene was hustle[d] into a movie – *The Golden Disc* (1958) – alon[g] with such contemporary pop performers a[s] Denis Lotis, Nancy Whiskey, Sheila Buxto[n] and disc-jockey David Jacobs.

Steele rejected rock; Vaughan became mor[e] of a housewives' choice; but Dene just was n[ot] cut out for the life. He was over-exposed an[d] harried to the point of nervous collapse. Calle[d] into the Army for two years' National Service[,] he found the pressure too much for him, an[d] was abruptly discharged. His career collapsin[g] under him, Dene turned to fervent stree[t] corner evangelism.

Bachelor boy

This confusion in British movie rock circles lef[t] space for Cliff Richard (b. 1940), who reall[y] was in the Presley mould, though his emer[-] gence – into a mixed world of successf[ul] movies and hit records – was by no mean[s] straightforward.

His career actually began in *Serious Charg[e]* (1959), directed by Terence Young, starrin[g] Anthony Quayle and Sarah Churchill. The fil[m] boasted a serious topic – an alleged sex offence[.] Richard had only a small role but, with a grou[p] of session musicians he also sang 'Living Do[ll]

The YEAR'S SMASH-HIT MUSICAL!

Lonnie DONEGAN
Dickie VALENTINE
Jim DALE
Petula CLARK
Russ HAMILTON
Joan REGAN

and many others in

6·5 SPECIAL

A FABULOUS ARRAY OF STARS IN ONE GREAT FILM!

ANGLO AMALGAMATED FILM DISTRIBUTORS LTD.

Above: life was cruel to Terry Dene, and even his star appearance in The Golden Disc *failed to guarantee success. Right:* 6.5 Special *moved from TV to film to encapsulate the frenetic rhythm of the whole beat era*

which Lionel Bart had written for the soundtrack. It was later recorded first as part of a movie-linked EP record, then put out as a single at a slower tempo and with Richard's own backing group – then The Drifters, now the Shadows. The single sold a million, and decisively changed his career from rocker to versatile all-rounder.

Expresso Bongo (1959) was a parallel key movie in the Cliff Richard story, a film version of a Wolf Mankowitz stage hit. Richard played Bongo Herbert, an up-and-coming singer, and one of his songs – 'Voice in the Wilderness' – was a huge hit, despite the star's intense dislike of it.

Cliff Richard's status in the area of rock-movie action grew steadily. *The Young Ones* in 1961 had him with The Shadows, Robert Morley and Carole Gray, plus a powerful score that included the hits 'Bachelor Boy' and 'Summer Holiday'. This film was publicized as 'the first film ever to have three tunes in the Top 10'. And Cliff gained even more credibility as a box-office draw with *Summer Holiday* (1963) directed by Peter Yates, featuring The Shadows, Una Stubbs, Lauri Peters and Melvyn Hayes.

You gotta have Faith

But events have surely proved that Adam Faith (b. 1940) – a vocal contemporary of the emergent Cliff – is the best actor of all the early British rock artists. His first film foray was *Beat Girl* (1960) co-starring with Shirley Ann Field. It contained the hit 'Someone Else's Baby', itself melodically emphasized by the pizzicato string backing laid down by John Barry. The film had Faith playing a beatnik kid in a storyline that earned it an X certificate, and he agreed with the critics that it was 'no epic'. It was banned in many territories: in Singapore, incidentally, because it showed a

young girl being rude to her parents.

Faith's second movie – *Never Let Go* (1960) with Richard Todd, Peter Sellers and Elizabeth Sellars – actually came out first, because at the time there was a queue of X-rated films waiting to get out on the cinema circuits. Faith has stuck with his acting, of course, on television as Budgie, in *Stardust* (1974), and more recently with Roger Daltrey in *McVicar* (1980).

Artful Anthony

As British celluloid rock sought acceptance at a reasonably serious level internationally, the Anthony Newley episode emerged to provide an element of farce. Newley (b. 1931) – an actor since he was 15, regularly in films, spotlit for playing the Artful Dodger in *Oliver Twist* (1948) – took on a character role in *Idle on Parade* (1959) as Jeep Jackson, a rock singer enlisted by accident into the British Army's crack regiment. For most Newley viewers this was the first time he had actually sung in public. From getting maybe one or two letters from fans a week as a respected actor, he got a hundred a day as a rock singer. Newley was then only 28.

Newley, of course, went seriously into the music world, collaborating with Leslie Bricusse, and inspiring big-stage successes like *Stop the World – I Want To Get Off*. Today he is a Las Vegas-based musical entertainer. But his entry into the rock world of 1959 and subsequent television exposure on shows like *6.5 Special* and *Drumbeat* were purely accidental.

And the stars wore jeans

The television success of *6.5 Special*, with its fast-paced format, led to a full-length cinema

production, out in 1958, and starring among many others the young Jim Dale. Dale (b. 1935) was another part-time British rock singer who figured in the movie scene of the late Fifties. He went on to work in the Carry On series, and had remarkable success as a stage actor both with Olivier's National Theatre and later on Broadway.

Actor-turned-singer John Leyton was showcased in the short *The Johnny Leyton Touch* (1961) and was another Presley successor who did not quite succeed, despite appearing briefly in *It's Trad, Dad!* (1962). This was predictably strong on traditional jazz (Chris Barber, Acker Bilk, Kenny Ball, The Temperance Seven), but also included the rock brigade, notably Craig Douglas, Chubby Checker and Gary Bonds from the USA. Joe Brown was another established pop name who showed potential in the whole crazy mixed up world of British teenage talent coming of age in movies good, bad and indifferent.

Many observers of the scene felt that Billy Fury should have been bigger than most. *Play It Cool* (1962) featured his moody aggression alongside Helen Shapiro, Danny Williams and one Shane Fenton, later to make the charts all over again as Alvin Stardust. And through the whole hectic era, Elvis Presley was turning out two or three movies a year, as regular as clockwork.

The Beatles, Dave Clark and the others were just around the corner. Ideas of presenting authentic British rock'n'roll music were to become creatively and dynamically more sound. But the first fumbling, stumbling efforts to get the music into cinematic formats will long be fondly remembered.   PETER JONES

The Wild One

Directed by Laslo Benedek, 1953

Prod co: Stanley Kramer Production, released by Columbia Pictures Corporation. **prod:** Stanley Kramer. **sc:** John Paxton, from story by Frank Rooney. **photo:** Hal Mohr. **ed:** Al Clark. **art dir:** Walter Holscher. **mus:** Leith Stevens. **r/t:** 79 minutes. Pre-release title *Hot Blood*.
Cast: Marlon Brando (*Johnny*), Mary Murphy (*Kathie*), Robert Keith (*Harry Bleeker*), Lee Marvin (*Chino*), Jay C. Flippen (*Sheriff Singer*), Peggy Maley (*Mildred*), Hugh Sanders (*Charlie Thomas*), Ray Teal (*Frank Bleeker*), John Brown (*Bill Hannegan*), Will Wright (*Art Kleiner*), Robert Osterloh (*Ben*), Robert Bice (*Wilson*), William Vedder (*Jimmy*), Yvonne Doughty (*Britches*), Keith Clarke (*Gringo*), Gil Stratton Jr. (*Mouse*), Darren Dublin (*Dinky*), Johnny Taragelo (*Red*), Jerry Paris (*Dextro*), Gene Peterson (*Crazy*), Alvy Moore (*Pidgeon*), Harry Landers (*GoGo*), Jim Connell (*Boxer*), Don Anderson (*Stinger*), Angela Stevens (*Betty*), Bruno VeSoto (*Simmonds*), Pat O'Malley (*Sawyer*).

If ever a film was appropriated by its audience, it was *The Wild One*. Essentially a troubled, middle-aged 'problem' picture, it addressed itself to a socially and morally concerned public. However, the audience that it actually reached was one whose very existence was unclear at the time – the rebellious young. For perhaps the first time the teenage and adolescent audience asserted itself by idolizing Brando and taking the film to its collective heart.

Stanley Kramer produced the film after a deal to supply a string of low-budget features was made with Columbia. Earlier films in the package had included *Death of a Salesman* (1951) and *The Member of the Wedding* (1953). *The Wild One* was conceived as a torn-from-the-headlines project, and presented as a chilling warning. The opening caption reads:

'This is a shocking story. It could never take place in most American towns – but it did in this one. It is a public challenge not to let it happen again.'

John Paxton's script was based on a magazine story by Frank Rooney, itself a thinly fictionalized version of an incident from the summer of 1947 when a bike-gang took over the Californian town of Hollister for an evening. Other similar raids followed and juvenile delinquency came to be identified as a new social menace. *The Wild One* was the first movie to comment directly on these social developments, although Jean Cocteau's *Orphée* (1950) had already exploited the image of black-leather-bikers for other ends.

It seems probable that Benedek and Paxton saw the project rather differently from Kramer. The film has little or none of the stridency of its opening caption, and in fact does little to impose 'drama' on its basic situation, preferring to concentrate on character, atmosphere and setting. Although the film-makers are highly critical of most of the small-town residents, they in no sense present Johnny as a hero. However, the accuracy of their observation of the bikers, and the sensitivity that they and Brando bring to the character of Johnny are such that they – perhaps unwittingly – pave the way for audiences to hero-worship.

The film is at pains to apportion blame evenly. The bikers, who come from nowhere and have no evident aim, are introduced as hooligans and thieves. Their arrival in the town is presented as an intrusion on its tranquillity, although local traders relish the prospect of extra business. The situation does not deteriorate until Chino's gang arrives, whereupon things escalate through vandalism, an attack on the town telephone exchange, random

Turned away from a motorcycle rally for their rowdy behaviour, the members of the Black Rebels Motorcycle Club steal a trophy and ride into a small town (1). Johnny, their leader, is attracted to Kathie, waitress in Bleeker's Cafe and daughter of the town cop Harry (2). Violence flares when a rival gang, led by Chino (3), comes into town. After a fight with Johnny (4) Chino picks on local resident Charlie Thomas (5) and is jailed. As night falls, gang members 'arrest' Thomas and lock him up alongside Chino (6), but his friends soon release him. Johnny finds some of the Black Rebels terrorizing Kathie (7) and drives her off to a quiet beauty spot where they talk (8). Thomas and his cronies manage to trap Johnny (9) but he escapes when Harry intervenes. After a thrown tyre-iron knocks him off his bike and the riderless machine mows down an elderly pedestrian (10), the state sheriff charges Johnny with murder. At first only Kathie pleads for him (11) but eventually two townsfolk are prepared to testify to his innocence. Released on trust, Johnny returns to the cafe and after presenting the stolen trophy to Kathie he rides off alone (12).

terrorizing of citizens and the accidental death of the old man. The local residents, on the other side, are sketched as grasping (Bleeker, the bar owner), cowardly and ineffectual (Harry, the cop), brutal and fascistic (Charlie Thomas and his posse of vigilantes) and lying (no-one comes forward to exonerate Johnny until the last minute).

This bleak view of the characters recalls Paxton's earlier script for Edward Dmytryk's *Crossfire* (1947) suggesting that *The Wild One*'s roots are closer to the *films noirs* of the Forties than to the liberal, conscience-pricking movies being made around the same time. As in a *film noir*, a faltering half-suppressed romance motif is the only element that alleviates the gloom. Johnny's liaison with Kathie is the film's main device for exploring his character, and it produces the exceptionally well-observed moment of Kathie's realization that Johnny is actually afraid of her.

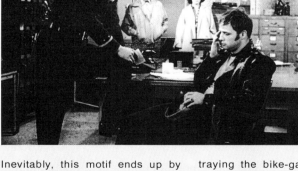

Inevitably, this motif ends up by sentimentalizing Johnny as a victim of society and of a lack of parental love, always failing to make successful heterosexual human contacts.

The Hungarian-born Benedek has been articulate about his aims: 'The subject isn't juvenile delinquency; it's youth without ideals, without goals, which doesn't know what to do with the enormous energy it possesses.'

His insistence on accurately portraying the bike-gang resulted in his spending time with actual bikers, even casting a number of them in the film. It also resulted in a musical score that broke new ground. Leith Stevens' music was the first consistently jazz-orientated score for a major feature, and the first score that was mainly integrated into the action from a visible juke-box or an off-screen radio.

A *Variety* reviewer in 1953 – impressed by the film's production values and by Brando's performance, but worried by 'the almost total exclusion of human decency' from the storyline – predicted that the film would prove 'hard to sell'. He was right as far as Britain was concerned; the British censor banned it until 1968. However, like most adults at the time, he failed to sense how Brando's charisma would allow his inarticulacy to speak volumes to a generation that had not yet found its own voice.

TONY RAYNS

47

With the advent of sound, films became less suitable for children's eyes and ears – partly owing to the language used but also to the increasing 'sophistication' of the visual image. In many countries, those concerned with the young began to realize that if children were to be given the entertainment they wanted, films would have to be made specially for them

The idea that children should be provided with specially devised and produced entertainment only began to take shape when films grew more exclusively adult in their subject-matter. Early films were mostly so simple that parents and children alike could appreciate them, and even into the Twenties most films presented few problems in entertaining the relatively young, although they might have needed whispered help in spelling out the dialogue captions – which were usually held on the screen long enough for even the slowest reader to absorb. However, it was in the Twenties that an increasingly adult content began to present problems of suitability. Censorship – which was not established in the United States until the early Thirties – then began to determine whether or not a child should be admitted to the cinema.

One of the first countries to establish studios specializing in making films for children and young people (as distinct from general films with a strong appeal for children, such as the Tarzan or Sherlock Holmes series) was the USSR, which was relatively free from a hard-line box-office policy that demanded self-paying productions with handsome profits. After the nationalization of its studios in 1919, the USSR established specialized production in order that young children – like their parents – should begin to understand the nature of the Revolution. The resulting films usually involved protagonists who were children, and as such would be readily identified with.

The USSR's policy was to place young graduates from the film schools under the supervision of established directors and then push them into immediate production – usually handling subjects with which they could themselves identify. One of the best known films made in this way was Vladimir Legoshin's *Byeleyet Parus Odinky* (1938, *Lone White Sail*), based on the adventures of a group of children during the Revolution. It was made by the Children's Film Studio of Moscow, established in 1936, which also produced Mark Donskoi's outstanding trilogy based on the life of Maxim Gorki: *Detstvo Gorkovo* (1938, *Childhood of Gorki*), *V Lyvdyakh* (1939, *My Apprenticeship*) and *Moi Universiteti* (1940, *My Universities*). Donskoi also made a virulently anti-Nazi film *Raduga* (1944, *The Rainbow*), with many children taking part in this study of resistance to the German invaders of a rural town. *The Rainbow* also involved scenes that might have been thought unsuitable for children; a soldier in the relief force that liberates the town shoots his wife who has become the self-indulgent mistress of the German commandant. Donskoi's special interest in children had made him very successful in eliciting remarkable performances from them.

Sergei Gerasimov, another highly regarded director attached to the pre-World War II Leningrad studios, also revelled in subjects involving youth. *Semero Smelykh* (1936, *The Seven Brave*), is about a party of youthful geologists in the Arctic while a celebrated

adolescent resistance group in Krasnodon is described in *Molodaya Gvardiya* (1948, *The Young Guard*), the film itself being largely made by young undergraduates. The USSR also produced newsreels – designed specially for children – under the Pioneer banner. Of the capitalist countries, the first off the mark with children's films was Japan, beginning in 1924.

Investing in the future

Production and distribution of such specialized films has always presented the problem of who is to pay for them in the first place, and how and where they can be effectively exhibited. In the USSR these films were considered to be part of the children's education and political indoctrination, and were suitably subsidized. In capitalist countries, the filmic entertainment of children was seen as insurance for future cinema attendance, and so thought to be good for the box-office in the long rather than the short term. Children by themselves were patently not likely to produce satisfactory box-office receipts on a scale capable of matching the expensive process of film production, let alone enabling any profit to be made. Ideally

Right: a gratifying sight for any children's film-maker – this infra-red picture was taken at the Regal Cinema, Harrow Road, London, in 1955. Top right: the badge owned by a vast army of Saturday matinée picturegoers

young eyes
only

BUSH CHRISTMAS

EAGLE-LION DISTRIBUTION

CHILDREN'S CINEMA CLUBS
GAUMONT
FOR BOYS AND GIRLS

Left: production shot from Skid Kids *(1953), in which children foil London's bicycle thieves. Above: Richard O'Sullivan and Jenny Jones in* Raiders of the River *(1956). Above right: a horse-rustling tale made in 1947*

children's films should be shown to child audiences alone, uninhibited by the presence of their elders. This led to the introduction of children's matinées, usually held on Saturday mornings when there was no school and the cinemas were not required for normal screenings. This step obviously called for a sizeable supply of special films which in turn meant the investment of considerable capital.

Gradually, after World War II, countries as diverse as Britain and India, as well as Japan and the USSR, became involved in the regular production of entertainment films for children. To these were soon added productions from the newly-established socialist countries, notably Czechoslovakia and Poland. Specialized studios were founded in Poland in 1950, in the German Democratic Republic in 1953 and Czechoslovakia in 1955, the same year in which India – with its large and highly profitable film industry – established its Children's Film Societies with government-financed backing.

British backing Britain

In Britain, the Children's Film Foundation (CFF) was established in 1951. The British film industry agreed to sponsor the independent, low-budget production of strictly entertainment films for young children, and so set up a non-profit making organization registered as a

49

Above: a poignant image from The Rainbow. *Below: potential for disaster in the Hungarian* Gyerekbetegfégek *(1966, Grimaces). Below right:* Friend or Foe *(1982) is a wartime story about two ten-year-old evacuees who find themselves indebted to a German soldier*

limited company without share capital. Since 1951 the British Film Production Fund has collected a levy allocating a proportion to the CFF, which is also subsidized by revenue from cinema distribution in the United Kingdom as well as from overseas sales. Today the CFF is still going strong, producing such films as *A Hitch in Time* (1979) and *Big Wheels and Sailor* (1980), and keeping its high standards in line with children's changing expectations. The CFF has also proved itself to be invaluable in the hunt for talent, and such well-known British actors and actresses as Susan George, Olivia Hussey, David Hemmings, Anthony Newley and Jean Simmons perhaps owe their careers to the British CFF.

Field studies

Prior to the CFF's inauguration, the Rank Organization had set up a special division to make films under the general direction of Mary Field, later to become the first director of the CFF. Mary Field, the author of *Good Company*, a study of the problems and opportunities facing film-makers involved in children's entertainment, was a specialist in child psychology and made a close study of the reactions of her young audiences to the films made for them. The scriptwriters and directors of the early films had to ensure that children were always active participants in and obvious instigators of the action; the children naturally had to be within the age-range of the audience; adults were normally kept in the background, often as characters whom the children could easily outwit; dialogue was usually kept to a minimum so as not to outpace easy acceptance by the youngest element; and the action had to be adventurous and exciting without posing too violent or heavy a threat to the young heroes

and heroines. Most features (or featurette lasted about an hour – the right span of time hold the concentrated attention of you audiences. In a normal programme the would be one film of this length, supported shorts in the form of serials or entertainin factual films.

Breaking the language barrier

Film-makers successful in the production films for children during the Seventies inclu the late Julian Bryan, founder of the Inte national Film Foundation in America. His filr consist of entertaining half-hour docume taries made in different parts of the worl using animation as well as live action. Or of his films was based on Big Nose, a popul Japanese puppeteer working in Tasmania. T Learning Corporation of America is perha more concerned with education, but films su as *Big Henry and the Polka Dot Kid* (1977), abo a child's care for an aged and sick dog, ar Peter Medak's *The Rocking Horse Winn* (1977), adapted from a story by D. H. Law rence, are basically entertainment film The U.S. also has the non-profit making Chil ren's Film and Television Foundation, esta lished in 1970, to entertain children in cinem on Saturdays in much the same way as tl British children's matinées. Faroun Films w founded in Montreal, Canada, in the Sixties. the late Seventies the Children's Film Socie movement in India had 105 films in dist bution, many acquired from overseas, and it interesting to note that children's entertai ment has always been international in order make the maximum use of every available a suitable film from countries interested in tl medium.

Festivals exclusively designed for children entertainment films have taken place fro time to time in both Europe and America. T American Film Festival has awards, rece winners being animated films adapted fro children's books such as Czechoslovakia *Streya Nonna* (1978), the American juven detective story *Nate the Great Goes Undercov* (1978), and Tom Davenport's Appalachia adaptations of a Grimm's fairytale *The Fr King* (1980).

However, in recent years – and perhaps as result of economic pressures and the increa ing sophistication of children – there is a f greater range and degree of adult skill ar interest to be found in the strictly education field of film-making than in the realms of pu entertainment.   ROGER MANVEI

THE APU TRILOGY

Apur Sansar, directed by Satyajit Ray, 1959
Prod co: Satyajit Ray Productions. **prod/sc:** Satyajit Ray, from the novel by Bibhutibhushan Bandapaddhaya. **photo:** Subrata Mitra. **ed:** Dulal Dutta. **art dir:** Bansi Chandragupta. **mus:** Ravi Shankar. **sd:** Durgadas Mitra. **r/t:** 106 minutes. Released in GB as *The World of Apu.*
Cast: Soumitra Chatterjee (*Apu*), Sharmila Tagore (*Aparna*); Sharpan Mukerjee (*Pulu*), S. Aloke Chakravarty (*Kajole*).

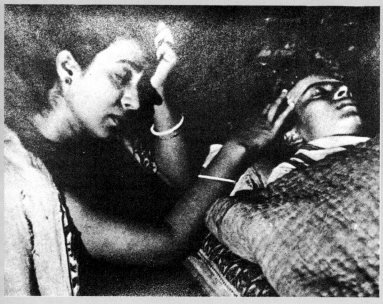

Pather Panchali, directed by Satyajit Ray, 1955
Prod co: Government of West Bengal. **prod/sc:** Satyajit Ray, from the novel by Bibhutibhushan Bandapaddhaya. **photo:** Subrata Mitra. **ed:** Dulal Dutta. **art dir:** Bansi Chandragupta. **mus:** Ravi Shankar. **sd:** Bhupen Ghose. **r/t:** 115 minutes. Released in the USA as *Song of the Little Road.*
Cast: Kanu Banerjee (*Harihar*), Karuna Banerjee (*Sarbojaya*), Uma Das Gupta (*Durga*), Subir Banerjee (*Apu*), Chunibala (*the aunt*).

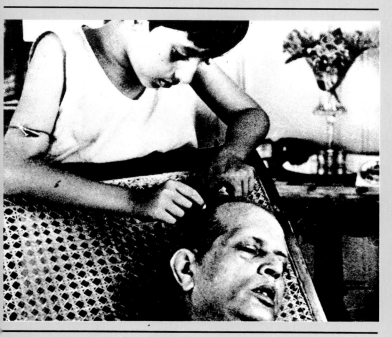

Aparajito, directed by Satyajit Ray, 1956
Prod co: Epic Films Private Ltd. **prod/sc:** Satyajit Ray, from the novel by Bibhutibhushan Bandapaddhaya. **photo:** Subrata Mitra. **ed:** Dulal Dutta. **art dir:** Bansi Chandragupta. **mus:** Ravi Shankar. **sd:** Durgadas Mitra. **r/t:** 113 minutes. Released in GB as *The Unvanquished.*
Cast: Pinaki Sen Gupta (*Apu*), Kanu Banerjee (*Harihar*), Karuna Banerjee (*Sarbojaya*), Subodh Ganguly (*the headmaster*), K.S. Pandey (*Pandey*), Ramani Sen Gupta (*the uncle*), Kali Charan Ray (*press proprietor*), Sudipta Ray (*Nirupama*), Smaran Ghosal (*Apu as an adolescent*), Charu Ghosh (*Nanda Babu*), Santi Gupta (*landlord's wife*), Ajay Mitra (*Anil*).

Of all the haunting visions evoked by the *Apu* trilogy, the cycle of life and death is the most striking. *Pather Panchali* (1955, *Song of the Little Road*), *Aparajito* (1956, *The Unvanquished*) and *Apur Sansar* (1959, *The World of Apu*) follow the fortunes of a small Indian family through three generations. It shares the same emotions, the same fears and joys as most rural, lower-middle-class families. Life and death go hand in hand, and even small hopes usually dwindle and die.

In *Pather Panchali* the father's elderly aunt looks forward to her next incarnation. In India, very old people are equated with children in that they must be cared for as they become less mobile and so lose their independence. As the aunt nears her death, she finds an affinity with young Durga who gives her stolen fruit to eat.

Durga and her brother Apu have been quarrelling, and as they reach a truce the scene is intercut with one in which the old lady is drinking water – considered to be an elixir of life – during her last moments. Her death finally unites the paralleled scenes and comes as quickly as the children's reconciliation.

As Durga enters her aunt's hut she is still lost in the memory of her first glimpse of a passing steam train and the fight with Apu. A fly is circling round her aunt's dead body as a candyman is heard advertising his wares outside. The sound is a poignant one for in India candy is forbidden after a family death until 13 days of mourning have been observed. As Durga looks at the body she suddenly sees herself as her aunt – an old, unwanted lady in a male-orientated society – and she is shocked by the thought.

A few years pass but Durga still enjoys teasing her brother. One day they are caught in a monsoon. Apu shelters but Durga allows herself to be drenched and becomes very ill. Ironically, the Durga puja – a ritual ceremony of worship to the goddess Durga – is being celebrated outside, and as the noisy festivities gradually fade out, so the life in Durga – named after the goddess – slowly drains away.

In the second part of the trilogy Harihar, Apu's father, also dies during a religious ceremony. Diwali – the festival of the triumph of good over evil – is being celebrated in the city of Benares and the noise of merriment carries to the house where Harihar and his son are talking. Apu's life seems to be opening up, full of hopeful prospects, but there is no such future for his father. Harihar is physically exhausted, and as the night deepens and the oil lamp flickers and goes out, he sinks into eternity.

The last part of the trilogy features the death of another of Apu's loved ones, this time his wife Aparna. She dies in childbirth and at first Apu rejects his son. However, as Apu comes to accept his child he accepts Aparna's death and becomes determined to help his son develop in a world which offers him great opportunities for advancement.

The trilogy is often compared to Donskoi's trilogy on the life of Maxim Gorky. Indeed, the director Satyajit Ray admits to Donskoi's influence in his work. However, Ray was also as much influenced by Sanskrit classics, such as Kalidasa's dramatic poem *Shakuntala*, as he was by the depiction of rural life in Flaherty's films and humanism in Renoir's.

51

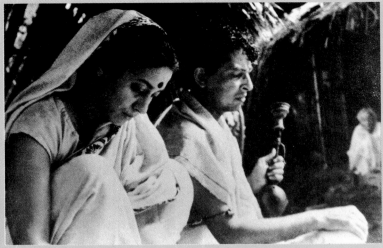

1

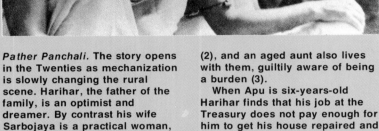

2

Pather Panchali. The story opens in the Twenties as mechanization is slowly changing the rural scene. Harihar, the father of the family, is an optimist and dreamer. By contrast his wife Sarbojaya is a practical woman, calmly confronting the everyday problems of existence (1). They have two children, Durga and Apu (2), and an aged aunt also lives with them, guiltily aware of being a burden (3).

When Apu is six-years-old Harihar finds that his job at the Treasury does not pay enough for him to get his house repaired and Apu is sent to a school for the poor. However, Harihar is offered extra money for performing a religious ceremony in another village and he leaves home, later sending word that he has gone on to Benares in search of more money. After the family has suffered a long period of hardship, Harihar returns with the money but finds his daughter Durga on her deathbed (4). Sarbojaya and Apu move with him to Benares in the hope of finding a better future.

Aparajito. Harihar makes his living by reciting scriptures on the banks of the Ganges (5). However the bustling life of the city proves to be overwhelming and he dies of exhaustion (6). Apu is raised by his mother who takes on work as a cook in order to support them (7).

5

6

9

10

Pather Panchali was made without any encouragement from Ray's contemporaries. Most Indian film-makers of the time were busy making films featuring a non-existent, synthetic society. Their argument for this was that the majority of people in India lead miserable lives of deprivation, and films – as the major medium of mass entertainment – should provide some kind of solace for their disillusionment. Ray refused to withdraw into such fantasies.

Inspired by the neo-realism of De Sica, Luchino Visconti and Roberto Rossellini, Ray based his script on Bibhutibhushan Bandapaddhaya's novel *Pather Panchali.* The story centres on a poor Bengali family and Ray brilliantly captures the beauty of the countryside, the grimness of poverty and the eternal fight for survival.

After gaining some experience in film-making on a visit to London, Ray started shooting *Pather Pan-* chali in October, 1952. By the time 5000 feet of film had been shot and rough cut the funds had run out. There followed long periods of enforced idleness while Ray peddled his incomplete film to every possible financier. Eventually the West Bengal government agreed to sponsor the completion of the film

4

Nevertheless, she has more ambitious plans for Apu and she decides to return to their old village so that Apu can be trained as a priest by his uncle.

However, Apu has other ideas and goes to university in Calcutta, working in the evenings to support himself. Meanwhile, his mother has grown weak and ill under the strain of her poverty-stricken life. When Apu comes home for the holidays he finds his mother dead and when he returns to Calcutta for his exams he decides to stay for good.

The World of Apu. Apu has ambitions to become a novelist and spends his days struggling to put his dreams into words. One day he attends a wedding (8) but during the ceremony it is revealed that the arranged marriage has been a trick, for the bridegroom is insane. Apu rescues the bride Aparna, marrying her himself (9), and gradually they fall in love. When Aparna becomes pregnant she leaves for her parents' house to wait for the birth.

Eventually Aparna's brother comes to tell Apu he has a son but that Aparna died in childbirth. It is another terrible blow for Apu and he tears up his manuscripts.

However, his son (10) soon restores his interest in life and together they search for a better future (11).

8

and three years after it had been begun *Pather Panchali* was finished.

The film's release also faced some problems, but once on show the perceptive audiences of West Bengal welcomed it as a reflection of their own way of life. After all, West Bengal has always been responsible for any social, political and cultural changes in the country.

When *Pather Panchali* was first shown at the Cannes Film Festival in 1956, there was a tremendous amount of prejudice against a film which was supposedly made in the realist tradition of *Ladri di Biciclette* (1948, *Bicycle Thieves*). The director François Truffaut walked out after a couple of reels, saying 'Europeanized and insipid'.

Nevertheless, *Pather Panchali*'s timeless images, along with Ravi Shankar's lyrical music, had a unique spontaneity. It was not a neo-realistic work, nor a work of the *nouvelle vague*; it was distinctive in its own way and as incomparable as the waters of the Ganges which flow unobtrusively through the hills and plains.　RAKESH MATHUR 11

1

2

The Great Adventure is the story of two boys who live with their father on a farm in central Sweden. They rescue a young otter from a fisherman (1) and manage to hide him away in a cage without their father's knowledge, secreting him in the attic of the farmhouse for a whole winter (2).

The otter has a huge appetite, and it strains the boys' ingenuity to keep him well fed without their parents discovering the truth (3). The otter seems to flourish under their care, but with the coming of Spring new instincts begin to assert themselves.

Anders, the elder boy, realizes this, and feels he must return the lively animal to the lake (4); besides, Kjell – the younger brother – lets their secret out.

The boys' great adventure is over; the otter needs his liberation, and the younger boy begins to understand this primeval principle of all natural behaviour as he watches the migratory birds returning from the south to re-establish their summer home in Sweden.

Directed by Arne Sucksdorff, 1953
Prod co: Sandrews. **prod:** Arne Sucksdorff. **ass prod:** Nils Gustav Orn. **sc/photo/ed:** Arne Sucksdorff. **mus:** Erik Larsson. **sd:** Nils Gustav Orn. **narr:** Norman Shelley. **r/t:** 73 minutes. Stockholm premiere, 29 September 1953. Released in USA as *The Great Adventure*.
Cast: Anders Norborg (*Anders*), Kjell Sucksdorff (*Kjell*), Holger Stockman (*Kvast-Emil*), Sigvard Kihlgren (*Bonden*), Arne Sucksdorff (*the father*).

The Great Adventure

Arne Sucksdorff developed his unique talent for creative nature cinematography in Sweden during the Forties. Living with his family on a remote farm, he brought the vision of a poet to the wildlife around him and the animals and birds became the principal actors in his films – the vixen and her cubs, the otter, the lynx, the rabbit and the hare, the owl and the gull – many of them natural predators on each other as well as being killers of the farm livestock.

These lively but wary creatures fulfil their natural instincts in their native environment all within sight of Sucksdorff's cameras. His observation of them accepts them exactly as they are, without any falsely imposed dramatization that tries to motivate them like human beings.

Sucksdorff was born in 1917 in Stockholm and during his childhood he explored the forests, establishing a relationship with animals such as foxes and otters, which he collected for his own small wildlife zoo. He went on to study natural history and art in Stockholm, and during the later Thirties studied theatre in Berlin under the celebrated German actor Rudolf Klein-Rogge.

After touring Italy, he returned with a series of photographs that won him a prize in a Swedish film magazine. The money enabled him to buy a film camera, graduate from still photography to movies and begin his career as a nature film-maker, starting in 1941 with the series of documentary shorts which were to establish his name.

Sucksdorff wanted nature and the animals to speak for themselves,

without human comment. His first major short, *En Sommarsaga* (1941, A Summer Tale), was made with his own money but the film was immediately adopted by Svensk Filmindustri and his subsequent work was financed by them. *En Sommarsaga* was a brief, lyrical study of forest life linked by the close observation of a fox-cub's expedition into the perplexing world of trees, flowers, birds, insects and animals – on all of which the summer sun plays with enchanting visual effect.

In 1942 Sucksdorff went to Swedish Lapland to make two films; *Vinden Från Väster* (The West Wind) – in which a Lap boy starts out on a great migration from the shelter of the valleys to the northern plains where his people spend the summer – and *Sarvtid* (Reindeer Time) – which showed the rounding up of the reindeer in autumn. Next, Sucksdorff moved to an island in the Baltic to study the community of seabirds for *Trut!* (1944, The Gull), showing the conflict between gulls, greediest of birds, and the peaceful guillemots. After *Trut!*, critics began to read human, even political fables into his films, seeing in the conflicts of nature a reflection of wartime Europe. However, *Gryning* (1944, Dawn) and *Skuggor Över Snön* (1945, Shadows Across the Snow) were much more lyrical, portraying the forest in all its varied moods.

Sucksdorff's last short film to deal with life in the Swedish forests was the one critics thought to be

Far left: Sucksdorff waits for a good shot. Right and below: despite the thin plot the film contains beautiful moments, as these wildlife scenes are interwoven with the adventure

most allegorical – *En Kluven Värld* (1948, A Divided World). The film showed the violence of predatory animal-life in harsh winter conditions; a fox captures a hare but an owl glides down on silent wings to snatch the prey for itself.

In 1947, Sucksdorff completely changed his subject with *Människor i Stad* (People of the City), an impression of life in Stockholm presented without commentary; it won him an Oscar and made him well-known outside Sweden. He went on to make several more films about people – going as far from his forest as India, including Kashmir – before returning to Sweden to make his first feature film *Det Stora Äventyret* (1953, The Great Adventure).

The British documentary director Basil Wright has said of him that he 'casts a calm and truthful eye on the realities of nature'. Sucksdorff did not reveal how he obtained his intimate shots of birds and animals, but cinematography of this kind requires infinite patience; he combined complete authenticity with astonishing revelation, and his subjects were always perfectly lit and composed. Often he would photograph pet animals whose familiarity with his presence enabled him to obtain close-ups without the use of a hide or remote-controlled camera.

The Great Adventure epitomized his vision of the relationship between human beings and the natural life around them. It took two years to complete. Sucksdorff appears as the wise and understanding father of two boys – the younger of the two actually being his son – who come to learn by experience that a wild animal will know instinctively what is best for him, accepting care during the hard winter months, but eager to escape and return to his natural habitat as soon as spring arrives. It would seem that Sucksdorff re-created his own boyhood through the youngsters, and although the life of man differs greatly from the life of the animals, Sucksdorff seems to feel that young children may be able, instinctively, to draw closer to the animals than adults can normally do.

Although Sucksdorff made other feature films centred around human beings, such as *En Djungelsaga* (1957, The Flute and the Arrow), shot in the Far East, and *Mit Hem är Copacabana* (1965, My Home is Copacabana), made while he was director of a film school in Brazil, his genius has been best expressed with wildlife, and *The Great Adventure* remains his masterpiece. ROGER MANVELL

Billy (David Bradley) in Kes (1969).

lent movies dictated that kids ould be seen but not heard. hen sound came along they ill didn't protest much at the ay cinema and society pushed em from pillar to post. But in e Fifties Lolita, James Dean and eir brothers and sisters at last gan to turn the screws on eir elders and betters . . .

the mid-Fifties, Andy Hardy had gone badly tray. In real life he was Mickey Rooney on e wrong side of 30, a former child star gulfed in divorces, money problems and erior pictures. On screen in 1958, Rooney ed to revive memories of tranquil com- unities and stable families in *Andy Hardy mes Home*, but there was no audience left for ch wholesomeness – the kids preferred Sal neo or Presley, and the parents stayed at me with TV. Even for Rooney, the film was a version; the last hurrah for Andy Hardy was ndwiched between *Baby Face Nelson* (1957) d *The Last Mile* (1959), apocalyptic B movies out punks who turned their hatred and their ns on a stupid, hypocritical society.

Louis B. Mayer, who had died in 1957, uld have been aghast But just as his MGM bes, Rooney and Judy Garland, had found saster and dismay as adults, so Hollywood's ealization of childhood could no longer stand to the facts of life. The plight of the unloved ild in art is as old as *Oliver Twist*, and movies e *The Kid* (1921) and *The Champ* (1931) had derstood that orphanhood, separation and a ild's distress could be milked for pity so long the child was eventually restored to a mfortable home, high-key lighting and a cure future. Even *Oliver Twist* ends with the undling in a nice home so that its readers ay forget the nightmare of Fagin and Bill kes.

hildhood in ruins

t to think of the David Lean film of *Oliver vist* (1948) is to recall its gloomy city and the rid evil of the underworld characters. Dic- ns' London was relevant in 1948 because so any cities were wastelands after the war and many children homeless and lost. Italian o-realism frequently observed the effects of cial breakdown on children. Who could

Above: Jackie Coogan – the orphan befriended by Chaplin in The Kid *– still wearing his lost, unwanted look three years later in* A Boy of Flanders *(1924). Below: Oliver (John Howard Davies) at the mercy of a vicious Bill Sikes (Robert Newton) in* Oliver Twist

forget the thorough plotting of the road from delinquency to death in De Sica's *Sciuscià* (1946, *Shoeshine*) or the woeful countenance of the son in *Ladri di Biciclette* (1948, *Bicycle Thieves*)? Most eloquent of all was Rossellini's *Germania, Anno Zero* (1947, *Germany, Year Zero*), in which a little boy is seen as the seed of fresh fascism in the rubble of post-war Berlin. Fred Zinnemann's *The Search* and Joseph Losey's *The Boy With Green Hair* (both 1948) showed that Americans too were aware of how grimly the war had dealt with children. In Losey's film, the pained face of Peter (Dean Stockwell) seems to be looking at mankind's final abandonment of hope or charity.

Bombed homes meant shattered families. So few pre-war movies had mentioned divorce, let alone the havoc it could leave in children's lives – yet in the Fifties society saw rapid increases in marital instability, as well as widespread prosperity, changed attitudes about sex and birth control, and a rising tide of rebellion among teenagers. Most of those strains need to be invoked to explain the impact of James Dean and rock'n'roll in the middle of the decade. Dean, in his early twenties, played a schoolboy in *Rebel Without a*

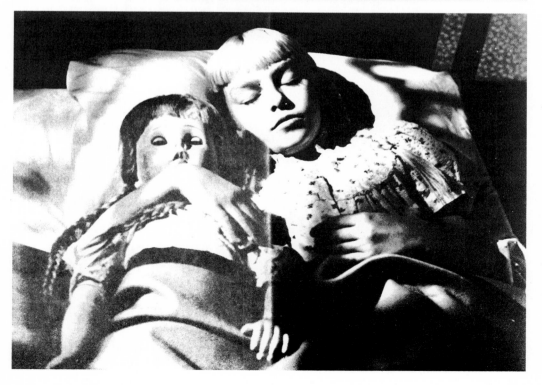

Cause (1955), but the movie reflected the confusing mixture of frustration, self-pity and independence in the young middle-class.

Lo and behold

After Dean's death, *The James Dean Story* (1957) – directed by the then unknown Robert Altman – used a mournful theme song, 'Let Me Be Loved', as if the single most marketable aspect of Dean was that the kid had been unloved. Ten years later, when the Rolling Stones howled about the dearth of satisfaction they were getting, it was apparent that love had become a more carnal preoccupation. But psychology was insisting that even infants had a sexual awareness, and the key novel of the Fifties – Nabokov's *Lolita* – concerns the seduction of an articulate, adult, would-be seducer by the plastic spirit of American childhood. Kubrick's 1962 movie of the novel nudges the love story into a 'respectable' student-professor affair: the movies still faced limits of censorship, and so we had to put up with Sue Lyon as Lo. Not until Jodie Foster played a pubescent hooker in *Taxi Driver* (1976) did the screen find an actress worthy of Nabokov's nymphet. Still, around 1960 there were many films sensitive to the dilemmas of children, and several that saw children as just young adults, sometimes as malign and wayward as their elders. The safeguards of sentimentality were being discarded, and no-one can have much hope of their being adopted again.

Young devils

In 1956, as if the system had suddenly glimpsed the sham of reiterated innocence and loveliness in children, it spewed up a picture – Mervyn LeRoy's far-fetched but nevertheless effective *The Bad Seed* – about a little witch (Patty McCormack), who kills anyone threatening to deprive her of an idiot mother's love. *Psycho* (1960) is a much better film, if no more believable. But at a mythic, psychological level, it depicts Norman Bates (Anthony Perkins) as an arrested child who has preserved his mother as a doll and as a She-who-must-be-obeyed. The notion that the child can harbour wickedness and be destructive has been very influential in movies: *The Exorcist* (1973) and *The Omen* (1976) constitute a reverse sentimentality in which the child has become a monster.

Linda Blair as the possessed girl in *The Exorcist* is as great a distortion as Shirley Temple. The best thing about the years around 1960 was the number of films that discovered children as human beings, less the emotional centres of their worlds than troubled observers of it. François Truffaut's *Les Quatre Cents Coups* (1959, *The 400 Blows*) was a key work in the French *nouvelle vague* and a reflection of Truffaut's own unhappy upbringing. Antoine Doinel (Jean-Pierre Léaud), the boy in the film, hardly realizes he is unloved, and Truffaut never lets him become an object of easy pathos.

Left: she's asleep – but what is she dreaming about? Patty McCormack as the young murderess in The Bad Seed. *Above left: James Mason as Humbert Humbert and Sue Lyon as the child-woman of his dreams –* Lolita. *Top: the legacy of war – bombsite boy Karel (Ivan Jandl) looks for his mother in* The Search *(left); Jean Seberg as a teenager pampered by her playboy father (David Niven) in* Bonjour Tristesse *(right)*

He is an ordinary kid – sly, cocky, bewildered,
abject – all within the space of a moment. It is
too good a picture to bear an obvious social
moral – it knows that chance decides so many
lives untouched by school or family. But when
it ends with a freeze-frame of the boy, escaped
from reform school but imprisoned in his
problem, the face stares out into the cinema as
if Truffaut wondered about lonely kids (like
himself) growing up in movie theatres and
shaped by the screen's illusions of romance
and transformation.

In Charles Laughton's *Night of the Hunter*
(1955), two children from a Grimm fairy tale
flee across a surreal landscape pursued by a
demon preacher (Robert Mitchum). Jean
Seberg plays a teenager in *Bonjour Tristesse*
(1958), who knows the turmoil of not being
able to give up her father for loves of her own.
The children in *Imitation of Life* (1959) suffer
from the ambitions and lies of their mothers. In
All Fall Down (1962) and *Hud* (1963), Brandon
De Wilde was very touching as a boy who
cannot decide which of his elders to believe
in. *The Courtship of Eddie's Father* (1963) introduced Ronny Howard – still earning a living
playing kids in the late Seventies – as the child
who has to deal with the loss of a parent. *To Kill
a Mockingbird* (1962) is a liberalizing view of
Southern bigotry rendered through the eyes of
children.

The Miracle Worker (1962) portrays a great
American heroine, but in the hands of Patty
Duke and Arthur Penn, who directed her as
the young Helen Keller, it is also the study of a
handicapped child poised between primitive
instinct and enlightenment. Hayley Mills made
her name in *Tiger Bay* (1959), where she
befriends a killer, and in *Whistle Down the Wind*
(1961), where she believes an escaping mur-
derer is Christ. From Japan, Nagisa Oshima's
Shonen (1969, *Boy*) shows a family that uses its
son as the 'victim' in fraudulent accident
claims. In *Mouchette* (1967), Robert Bresson
chose a young girl to represent the human
spirit confronted by suffering and resignation.
A High Wind in Jamaica (1965) – from the
Richard Hughes novel – shows kidnapped
children proving more cold-blooded than
pirates.

Spoonfuls of sugar
Of course there was also *Mary Poppins* (1964)
and *The Sound of Music* (1965), both triumph-
ant at the box-office and loyal to the Victorian,
paternalistic view of children. But an audience
needs such reassurances, especially if it is
learning how quickly the legendary innocence
of children can turn into the tribal fury of *Lord
of the Flies* (1963). Film had freed children from
many restrictions: they could be victims now,
beyond the reach of happy endings or
comfortable explanation. But, in recompense,
they had acquired a new energy that could
sometimes rebuke and victimize the older
world.   DAVID THOMSON

*Right: there is no escaping the look of
accusation – the unloved Billy (David Bradley)
and his only solace, the kestrel hawk he tends
and trains, in* Kes *(1969). Above right: Alan
Barnes, Diane Holgate and Hayley Mills as the
children who bring food to a convict hiding in a
barn, believing him to be Jesus, in* Whistle
Down the Wind. *Top right: Tetsuo Abe as the
victim of selfish, merciless parents in Oshima's*
Boy – *a harsh indictment of family traditions*

la Titanus presenta un film

di **ERMANNO OLMI**

OPERA PRIMA
ALLA XXII MOSTRA DI VENEZIA
PREMIO CITTÀ DI IMOLA COPPA 1961
PREMIO O.C.I.C.

IL POSTO

Directed by Ermanno Olmi, 1961
Prod co: The 24 Horses. **prod:** Alberto Soffientini. **sc:** Ermanno Olmi. **photo:** Lamberto Caimi. **ed:** Carla Colombo. **art dir:** Ettore Lombardi. **sd:** Giuseppe Donata. **r/t:** 90 minutes. Released in the USA as *The Sound of Trumpets* and in GB as *The Job*
Cast: Sandro Panzeri (*Domenico Cantoni*), Loredana Detto (*Antonietta*), Tullio Kezich (*psychologist*).

'I make films which tell stories about that part of human society which I have lived in,' says Ermanno Olmi. His feature-length documentary *Il Tempo si è Fermato* (1959, *Time Stood Still*) had been made as a result of his working for Edison-Volta, a Milan-based electrical company which was building a dam in a remote mountain area. In 1960, while still employed by the company but by then director of its film section, Olmi found a group of friends in Milan and later a distributor in Rome who made it possible for him to write and direct his first fiction film, *Il Posto*. It was inspired by his experiences as a clerk during his early years at Edison-Volta.

Inevitably the film was full of autobiographical observation and Olmi hotly rejects accusations that he made the almost-Dickensian atmosphere of that office too sad. He insists that office life in the Milan of the post-war years even in such a modern, American-styled firm as Edison-Volta was just like that. 'I remember that my first job in the office was to put numbered papers into numerical order,' says Olmi. As for the final 'musical chairs' over the vacant desk, he reports that clerks were always fighting over such idiotic things as who was to get the new issue of files or pencils. 'I was not a model clerk.' he adds.

Instead he was to become a model film-maker. *Time Stood Still* had won him prizes at documentary festivals but was neglected by the international art-cinema circuits. *Il Posto*, shown at the Venice Film Festival in 1961 at the same time as Pasolini's first film *Accattone* (1961), won Olmi many plaudits, and the Sutherland Trophy at the London Film Festival the same year. But by 1964 it had made only 150 million lire in Italy (about £80,000 at the time). Olmi divided the critics in his homeland and was often accused of being too much of a pessimist, allegedly because of his Christian vision of the world – which was in fact far from being that of a conformist Catholic. The left-wing film magazine *Cinema Nuovo* said he lacked a critical view of the **8**

Milanese capitalist society he was depicting and that he was a bad storyteller. The Catholic-orientated *Bianco e Nero*, on the other hand, complimented Olmi for the way he turned simple facts and observations into a 'well-composed narrative'.

By the beginning of the Sixties, neo-realism was widely thought to be finished as a style and as a method of film-making; but Olmi showed that what he had learned from the neo-realists – above all, from Rossellini – was still valid. However, nothing in *Il Posto* was improvised in terms of style. Though some of his friends were given credits for the photography on this and his other early films. Olmi himself always had firm control over the camerawork and editing. What he took from his neo-realist masters was an aptitude for capturing the simple facts of daily life. This was close to the concepts of Cesare Zavattini, the well-known screenwriter, who thought that the ideal film would simply set down everyday experience exactly as it was. For instance, the long and melancholy sequence of the New Year's party would seem like a documentary if it were not for the compassion that Olmi brings to his observation.

The neo-realist lesson also showed in his use of non-professional actors. Sandro Panzeri played Domenico with a simplicity reminiscent of Buster Keaton, but he was not to succeed in a professional career. Loredana

Detto never had any ambitions as an actress. Some time later, when Olmi sought her out to play a role in a colleague's film, the new meeting between them led to their marriage. For the part of the IQ-test interviewer, Olmi chose a friend, the writer and critic Tullio Kezich, who was to collaborate later on the script of *I Recuperanti* (1970, *The Scavengers*).

Il Posto differed from many other films of the Sixties that also apparently inherited the traditions of neo-realism, not only in the sophisticated style that Olmi revealed in his first attempt at film narrative but also in its wry humour, which is perhaps what made it so popular outside Italy. Most Italian comedy was then, as it still is, raucous and very Latin in spirit. Olmi's warm human feeling was more immediately recognizable as part of universal human experience. Sandro Panzeri was not to become the new Italian comic star of the Sixties, as so many critics had prophesied at the time; his face remained identified with that of Domenico. That last frozen-frame image of the boy sitting at his new desk in the grim Milan office where he had at last been appointed to his *posto*, his job for life, was to be unforgettable. Perhaps by now Domenico has moved up to the front desk. Olmi moved away altogether from his office desk in Milan and has made for himself a *posto* in Italian society as one of its most respected contemporary artists.
JOHN FRANCIS LANE

5

2

4

Early one cold winter morning, 17-year-old Domenico takes a train to nearby Milan (1), where he hopes to obtain a post with one of the big firms that offer security for life. When he arrives for his interview (2), Domenico and the other job-seekers are sent to a classroom (3). The first 'exam' they have to take is in maths. In the lunchbreak Domenico makes friends with another applicant, Antonietta (4). They eat a sandwich and stroll around Milan (5). She says a raincoat in a shop window would suit him. Back at the office, after an IQ test, Domenico is promised a job. When he returns home singing merrily, he finds the family silent and sullen at supper (6). His first job is as an office boy; he has to wear a uniform and run errands (7). He would like to show Antonietta that he bought the raincoat (8) but he never sees her. He goes alone to the office New Year's party (9). When he is promoted to an office desk, the other clerks move forward a place and he takes the desk at the back of the room (10).

7

10

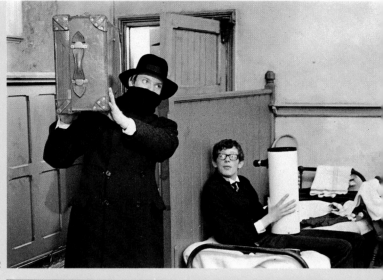

Which side will you be on?

if....

Paramount Pictures Presents
A MEMORIAL
ENTERPRISES FILM
Directed by
LINDSAY ANDERSON
Screenplay by
DAVID SHERWIN
Produced by
MICHAEL MEDWIN &
LINDSAY ANDERSON
Colour

ARTHUR LOWE · PETER JEFFREY · MONA WASHBOURNE · GEOFFREY CHATER · ANTHONY NICHOLLS
MALCOLM McDOWELL · RICHARD WARWICK · CHRISTINE NOONAN · DAVID WOOD · ROBERT SWANN

PARAMOUNT the cinema FROM THURSDAY
PICCADILLY CIRCUS Tel: 839.6494 downstairs DECEMBER 19TH

Appearing when it did, at the end of a year of youthful dissidence and revolt, *If . . . .* has often seemed to be a film made purposely to reflect the revolutionary fervour of the late Sixties. The truth is quite different.

Sometime in 1966, I had a telephone call from a friend of mine, the director Seth Holt. Seth asked if I would be interested in the idea of directing a film with him as producer. He explained that John Howlett, a young writer with whom he had been working, had shown him a script about life in an English public school. John had written it with David Sherwin with whom he had shared horrific years at Tunbridge School. Seth had not felt competent to undertake such a subject as he had not been to public school himself.

I responded to the story, then entitled *Crusaders*, because I approved of its romantic and rebellious spirit, and because there was so much of my own experience that could relate directly to the subject; and not just my experience of school but my experience of society in the years that had followed. So from the beginning the making of *If . . . .* was a warmly and intimately personal experience.

I met John and David and liked them. As soon as they realized that I had no wish to 'tone down' their story, they were responsive to my ideas.

It was David who undertook the work of revising the script with me. He and I took *Crusaders* to pieces, invented some new characters,

new incidents and a new structure. We decided that we wanted to make a film in 'epic' style which would aim consciously at the dignity and importance of a general theme. I had early on started elaborating the idea of an apocalyptic finale, but as the script developed we were anxious from the beginning *not* to appear to be reflecting revolutionary student action in France or America. The only element of contemporary iconography to be seen in the film is a poster of Che Guevara: it had been pinned up on the wall by a boy at the school where we were shooting. I did not have the heart to take it down.

Seth Holt did not in the end produce the film. His own director's career suddenly reanimated itself – and anyway I do not think he really liked the direction in which David and I took the script. This was away from naturalism and towards a style which I would certainly claim to be realistic ('realism' implying a concern with essences rather than with surfaces) and poetic rather than 'fantastic'.

I am often asked how we managed to find the actors for *If . . . .*, and particularly Malcolm McDowell. At first I thought that perhaps the script called for boys of exactly the age of the characters. But after some experiment, I realized that youth for the screen was a matter of temperament and character rather than of literal years. I remember vividly Malcolm's second audition on the stage of the Shaftesbury Theatre,

when he and Christine Noonan improvized with a marvellous, reckless intensity their love-hate scene in the Packhorse Café. They cast themselves in an instant.

Other key talents in *If . . . .* brought the blessing of familiarity. Arthur Lowe had given a fine performance in *This Sporting Life* (1963) and I had worked with Mary MacLeod, Graham Crowden and Jocelyn Herbert, the art director, at the Royal Court Theatre. Miroslav Ondříček, whom I had first met shooting for Miloš Forman when I visited Prague in the early Sixties, had been my cherished collaborator on *The White Bus* (1968).

It was hard to get the money to make *If . . . .*; it has always been

hard to get money for any British film of originality and risk. Eventually Albert Finney and Michael Medwin, who had started their own production company, Memorial Enterprises Ltd, out of Albert's rewards for *Tom Jones* (1963), managed to impress Charles Bluhdorn, the idiosyncratic head of Paramount Pictures, and we secured his backing. It was generally imagined by everyone that our subject was 'too English' to appeal outside the British market. In the event, although the picture was enthusiastically received by the British critics, it did only averagely decent business in the U.K. It was in the United States, in the rest of Europe and even behind the Communist frontiers that

College House. Return. College reassembles for the Winter Term. The boys of College House inspect lists, find their places and unpack their things. New boys, like Jute and Biles, are 'scum'. Authority among the boys is represented by four prefects known as 'whips' (1) including the impeccable Rowntree and the puritanical Denson. Mick Travis, a senior boy, arrives wearing a scarf to hide the moustache grown in the holidays (2). He and his friends, Johnny and Wallace, have little respect for tradition. College. College settles down to a routine. Chapel. Learning.

Games. Jute is grilled until he is word-perfect in the obligatory slang. Mick covers his study walls with images of freedom and violence. Dreaming, he listens to primitive music on his record-player. Biles is hunted, captured (3) and strung upside-down in the lavatory.

Term time. Bobby Philips, Rowntree's attractive scum, serves tea to the whips. In his study, Johnny leafs through magazines while Wallace peers into the mirror for symptoms of decay and Mick writes notes for a philosophical credo. 'Violence and revolution are the only pure acts' (4).

Ritual and romance. Bobby is repelled by Denson's yearning for him. Enthralled, he watches Wallace perform on the horizontal bar in the gym; a friendship is formed. During a College match, when they should be 'cheering loudly', Mick and Johnny escape downtown, pinch a motor-bike, and ride off to adventure and excitement with the girl at the Packhorse Café (5) (a black-and-white sequence).

Discipline. Mick, Johnny and Wallace are told by Rowntree that they have become a bad example to the House. They are beaten (6).

Resistance. The pressures of authority mount. The three boys mingle blood in a ceremony of solidarity.

Forth to war. During a College Cadet Corps field exercise, Mick shoots and bayonets the chaplin. The Headmaster gives the rebels a last chance: the Privilege of Service. They discover a forgotten stack of ammunition while clearing out lumber from under the stage (7).

Crusaders. Speech Day. General Denson is addressing boys and parents when the hall goes up in smoke. The assembly pour out into the Quad (8), to be met by a hail of bullets. The rebels have installed themselves, with automatic weapons, on the roof. Bravely, the Headmaster steps forward. 'Trust me! . . .' he cries (9). The girl takes steady aim. The Establishment counter-attacks. Mick continues firing (10) . . .

Directed by Lindsay Anderson, 1968.
Prod co: Memorial Enterprises Ltd. **prod:** Michael Medwin, Lindsay Anderson. **sc:** David Sherwin, from a story by David Sherwin, John Howlett. **photo** Eastman Colour): Miroslav Ondříček. **ass photo:** Chris Menges. **ed:** David Gladwell. **art dir:** Jocelyn Herbert. **mus:** Mark Wilkinson. **sd:** Christian Wangler. **ass dir:** John Stoneman. **r/t:** 111 minutes.
Cast: Malcolm McDowell (*Mick*), David Wood (*Johnny*), Richard Warwick (*Wallace*), Christine Noonan (*the girl*), Rupert Webster (*Bobby Phillips*), Robert Swann (*Rowntree*), Hugh Thomas (*Denson*), Michael Cadman (*Fortinbras*), Peter Sproule (*Barnes*), Peter Jeffrey (*Headmaster*), Anthony Nicholls (*General Denson*), Arthur Lowe (*Mr Kemp*), Mona Washbourne (*matron*), Mary MacLeod (*Mrs Kemp*), Geoffrey Chater (*Chaplain*), Ben Aris (*John Thomas*), Graham Crowden (*History teacher*), Charles Lloyd Pack (*classic master*), John Garrie (*music master*). Tommy Godfrey (*school porter*), Guy Ross (*Stephans*), Robin Askwith (*Keating*), Richard Everitt (*Pussy Graves*), Brian Pettifer (*Biles*), Michael Newport (*Brunning*), Charles Sturridge (*Markland*), Sean Bury (*Jute*).

it had its greatest impact and greatest effect. If only the British distributors could understand that it is not necessarily by 'international elements' in casting or in a script that a film can transcend the limitations of provincialism or parochialism. It is by the vitality of emotional impulse, the urgency and importance of what needs to be said. This is a truth which Americans seem to recognize, alas, much more readily than the English. But then, Americans are less scared and more stimulated by challenge.
LINDSAY ANDERSON

1

2

3

The Aborigine and the girl 30,000 years apart ...together

WALKABOUT

Just about the most different film you'll ever see

Filmed in its entirety in the Australian wilderness.

20th Century Fox presents A MAX L. RAAB-SI LITVINOFF PRODUCTION WALKABOUT starring JENNY AGUTTER · LUCIEN JOHN DAVID GUMPILIL executive producer MAX L. RAAB produced by SI LITVINOFF directed and photographed by NICOLAS ROEG screenplay by EDWARD BOND based on the novel by JAMES VANCE MARSHALL music by JOHN BARRY COLOR BY DE LUXE

Walkabout was to have been the first film directed by Nicolas Roeg, who had established himself by the mid-Sixties as one of Britain's leading cameramen for his work on such films as *The Caretaker* (1963), *Nothing But the Best, The Masque of the Red Death* (both 1964), *Fahrenheit 451* (1966) and *Far From the Madding Crowd* (1967). Roeg became fascinated by James Vance Marshall's novel, visited Australia to research settings and locations, and persuaded playwright Edward Bond to construct a screenplay. But the project then had to be shelved for lack of production support, and Roeg instead teamed up with Donald Cammell to make his joint directing debut with *Performance* (1970).

At first glance the two subjects could hardly look more different. *Performance*'s fetishistic study of a small-time London crook's metamorphosis in the claustrophobic home of a retired pop-star has little obvious connection with a trek through the Australian desert. But *Performance* too is about the fortuitous collision of opposites, their possible interaction and exchange, their final severance; and as it happens, the summary applies equally (with small variations) to Roeg's following films – *Don't Look Now* (1973), *The Man Who Fell to Earth* (1976) and *Bad Timing* (1980). It's all there in *Walkabout*, where the collision is both human (the white girl, the black Aborigine) and cultural (the city versus the outback); the interaction is a matter of both geographical and biological necessity (the girl is helpless in the aborigine's environment, as he would be in hers); and the severance is an inevitable consequence of two highly contrasted origins.

Roeg establishes the contrasts from the film's opening shots in which the bustling city is invaded b glimpses of the desert, until, with track from brick wall to ope ground, he permits the wilderness to take over completely. At the en of *Walkabout* the pattern is rever sed, with the invasion of the land scape by half-formed buildings discarded equipment (the little bo actually sets an abandoned trolle in motion once more), and at las the city crowds themselves. As result of Roeg's intercutting, cit and desert appear symbiotic, eac growing from the other; if the city dwellers look disconcertingly lik flowing sand, the wasteland, wit its exotic wildlife, is also seen t have a teeming social structure, i which experience is the vital part o survival. Nature and civilizatio may be opposites, but they have th same roots, the same needs, an Roeg's examination of those need reveals with each fresh illustratio the special, even lethal, price tha they demand.

The 'walkabout', explained in a opening title as an Aborigina custom, is accordingly an edu cation shared by the children o both cultures. For each, it provide the training for survival in a hostil environment. The Aborigine mus learn how to find water, to ki lizards, to cook kangaroo meat. Th girl, whom we first encounter in classroom, must learn elocutio etiquette, and *haute cuisine*; edu cation pursues her and her brothe as they carry the radio on thei journey, and ineffectual as its con tribution may seem when there i no water, the measured tones o technology continue to echo acros the outback long after the way hom has become clear again and thei brief benefactor has been left hang ing from a tree. 'I can multiply 84 b 84', the six-year-old announce proudly to the smiling savage fo

8

9

4

5

whom such skills are irrelevant; at the time, it seems incongruous, but it is the boy who lives and the Aborigine who dies.

Walkabout ends with the girl in her kitchen (as her mother was at the film's beginning). A voice speaks A. E. Housman's lines about 'the land of lost content . . . where I went and cannot come again' and we see a possibly remembered, possibly imagined bathing sequence with the girl, her brother and the Aborigine. Much enhanced by John Barry's soaring orchestration, this scene is a richly sentimental idyll, artificial enough to be subtly unconvincing. The viewer is invited to recognize through it that while simplicity has many obvious attractions, and that nature specializes in simplicities, they are awesomely transient. The 'walkabout' provided the justification for the partnership and at the same time its limit; despite the many

erotic half-promises between boy and girl (and much of *Walkabout*'s fascination comes from the delicacy with which it conveys their awareness of each other), they have no conceivable future together – which is why, having witnessed the gratuitous slaughter of wildlife by two white gunmen in a jeep, the Aborigine rises like a

skeleton from a landscape littered with bones to pay despairing homage to the female who has no further use for him. His time is past, even though Roeg's dislocated editing serves as a reminder that fragments of time, like bits and pieces of our upbringing, remain deeply embedded in the memories of us all.   PHILIP STRICK

Directed by Nicolas Roeg, 1971
Prod co: Max L. Raab – Si Litvinoff Films (Pty) Ltd (20th Century-Fox). **exec prod:** Max L. Raab. **prod:** Si Litvinoff. **assoc prod:** Anthony J. Hope. **sc:** Edward Bond, from the novel by James Vance Marshall. **photo** (Eastman Colour)**:** Nicolas Roeg. **sp photo:** Tony Richmond. **ed:** Anthony Gibbs, Alan Patillo. **prod des:** Brian Eatwell. **art dir:** Terry Gough. **mus:** John Barry. **add mus/songs:** 'Electronic Dance' by Billy Mitchell, 'Gasoline Alley' by Rod Stewart, 'Los Angeles' by Warren Marley, 'Hymnen' by Karl-Heinz Stockhausen. **sd rec:** Barry Brown. **sd re-rec:** Gerry Humphreys. **r/t:** 100 minutes. **Cast:** Jenny Agutter (*girl*), Lucien John (*brother*), David Gulpilil (*Aborigine*), John Meillon (*father*), Peter Carver (*no-hoper*), John Illingsworth (*husband*), Barry Donnelly (*Australian scientist*), Noelene Brown (*German scientist*), Carlo Manchini (*Italian scientist*).

A teenage girl and her brother are taken for a drive in the Australian bush by their father. As she lays out the picnic, the father suddenly produces a pistol (1) and starts shooting; when the children take cover, he shoots himself. Reassuring her brother that it is nothing serious, the girl leads him away into the desert (2). By nightfall they are completely lost.

Next day they find an oasis – but soon the water is gone and their situation looks desperate (3). Unexpectedly an Aborigine youth appears out of the desert (4); he is on his 'walkabout' – the six-month period in the wilderness which, by tribal custom, will establish his manhood. He takes them under his protection and guides them through the vast wasteland (5).

At last they reach an abandoned homestead (6) which seems a natural place for them to stay. But the Aborigine then takes the boy (7) and shows him a nearby highway that could lead the way back to civilization. Disturbed that he and the girl may shortly have to part company, the Aborigine paints himself and begins a dance of courtship (8); the girl retreats from him in terror (9), fearing violence of some kind. He continues the ritual for hours, past the point of exhaustion, and in the morning they find him dead (10). Seemingly unconcerned, they take the road back to safety, only to be greeted with hostility at the first town they reach (11).

Years later, the girl receives her husband home from the office. As he chatters of minor triumphs in his business affairs, she recalls a time when three children swam together in the sunlit waters of a far-distant lake.

7

11

THE LAST PICTURE SHOW

On its first appearance in 1971, *The Last Picture Show* had a potent effect on audiences everywhere. This evocative depiction of small-town life, recalled with such affection and loving detail, seemed like the kind of film that American cinema had well-nigh stopped producing for twenty years or more.

Reduced to a mere synopsis, the incidents depicted could easily appear no more than a slice of life from some Texan Peyton Place. But in Peter Bogdanovich's hands they unerringly convey the lost dreams, foolish aspirations and rivalries – the whole texture of life in a community in decline with not much of a remembered past and scant hope for a future. Chekhovian is the word which, without hyperbole, springs to mind.

All the film's adolescent sexual encounters bring their attendant disappointments and pain, but there is the wry implication that, with the passing years, nostalgia may well turn the pain into a treasured memory, so blur its edges that it can even be recalled with comfortable ruefulness as the one great chance that was missed. Thus it is that Sam the Lion, in the only long speech in the film, waxes lyrical to Sonny, as he fishes, about an idyllic moment from his youth when he and a girl

went swimming in the nude. The object of these reminiscences is by now a cynical fading beauty, alienated from her husband, capable of caustically advising her own daughter to do something about losing her virginity. She, too, clings to this long-ago attachment as her big moment: 'I guess if it wasn't for Sam, I'd just about have missed it, whatever it is,' she muses. The young folk, meanwhile, are amassing similar double-edged experiences to be nurtured and mellowed in memory's chest.

Bogdanovich's approach to his characters' shallow lives is never sentimental and often slyly humorous. Sitting in the tacky cinema, watching Minnelli's *Father of the Bride* (1950), Charlene removes her chewing-gum to kiss Sonny absently, fatuously absorbed in the never-never-land problems of Spencer Tracy coping with Elizabeth Taylor's coy pre-nuptial tantrums; later, in the last film to be shown before the cinema's closure (Hawks' *Red River*, 1948), John Wayne's herds making their impressive progress across the great prairies are a far cry indeed from the forlorn tumbleweed encroaching on this dying township where the only cattle seen are crowded in the back of a truck. The film clips

make their point as opiates, unquestioned grist to the fantasy mill which, with the demise of the old cinema, will now be supplied with coarser fodder by the new monster, television.

Already, in his first feature, *Targets* (1967), Bogdanovich had revealed an exceptional capacity for directing his actors and here he consolidates it. In the meticulously observed cramped interiors and grey exteriors (the whole film was shot in Archer City in north Texas) everyone finds his unobtrusive, unstarry place, superbly served by Robert Surtees' expressive black-and-white camerawork. For here is a film not so much shot in black and white but conceived in shades of those colours, best able to capture the period and the elegiac mood.

It seems perfectly natural that Ruth Popper should reward a spontaneous gesture of kindness from Sonny by inviting him into her kitchen for a drink; equally natural that the same neglected, middle-aged wife should entreat him to stay with her a little longer. A flutter of unrest clouds his face for a moment until the adolescent, himself in a state of emotional unrest, finds himself responding sympathetically to an older frustration he dimly apprehends. Their subsequent affair seems perfectly plotted and Ruth's transition from drabness to radiance and thence to shrill virulence when Jacy lures Sonny away from her is most movingly achieved by Cloris Leachman. All the relationships bear the same stamp of truth.

Bogdanovich's film is, in the Chekhovian sense, a comedy of empty lives where the characters occasionally go to ludicrous lengths to assert the fact that their existence is notable and their actions of importance. Jacy's bid for acceptance by the rich set is made by stripping naked on a diving board; she incites her mother's lover to rape her, and her elopement with Sonny, she hopes, will make her the talk of the town and provide her with a colourful *rentrée* to her final year in high-school.

The Last Picture Show has about it that kind of purity of expression that only the very greatest directors – Donskoi, Ford, Mizoguchi, Satyajit Ray – are able to sustain consistently throughout their careers. Most achieve it only once. It is one of those films whose characters linger in the memory, and that is happily re-seen time and time again.

DEREK PROUSE

Directed by Peter Bogdanovich, 1971
Prod co: A BBS Production/Last Picture Show Productions for Columbia. **exec prod:** Bert Schneider. **prod:** Stephen J. Friedman. **assoc prod:** Harold Schneider. **sc:** Larry McMurtry, Peter Bogdanovich, based on the novel by Larry McMurtry. **photo:** Robert Surtees. **ed:** Donn Cambern. **prod des:** Polly Platt. **art dir:** Walter Scott Herndon. **mus:** 1951 recordings by Hank Williams, Bob Willis and His Texas Playboys, Eddy Arnold, Eddie Fisher, Phil Harris, Pee Wee King, Hank Snow, Tony Bennett, Lefty Frizzell, Frankie Laine, Johnnie Ray, Johnny Standley, Kay Starr, Hank Thompson, Webb Price, Jo Stafford. **sd:** Tom Overton. **ass dir:** Robert Rubin, William Morrison. **prod man:** Don Guest. **r/t:** 118 minutes. Premier, New York Film Festival 1971. **Cast:** Timothy Bottoms (*Sonny Crawford*), Jeff Bridges (*Duane Jackson*), Cybill Shepherd (*Jacy Farrow*), Ben Johnson (*Sam the Lion*), Cloris Leachman (*Ruth Popper*), Ellen Burstyn (*Lois Farrow*), Eileen Brennan (*Genevieve*), Clu Gulager (*Abilene*), Sam Bottoms (*Billy*), Sharon Taggart (*Charlene Duggs*), Randy Quaid (*Lester Marlow*), Joe Heathcock (*sheriff*), Bill Thurman (*Coach Popper*), Barc Doyle (*Joe Bob Blanton*), Jessie Lee Fulton (*Miss Mosey*), Gary Brockette (*Bobby Sheen*), Helena Humann (*Jimmie Sue*), Loyd Catlett (*Leroy*), Robert Glenn (*Gene Farrow*), John Hillerman (*teacher*), Janice O'Malley (*Mrs Clarg*), Floyd Mahaney (*Oklahoma patrolman*), Kimberley Hyde (*Annie-Annie Martin*), Noble Willingham (*Chester*), Marjory Jay (*Winnie Snips*), Joye Hash (*Mrs Jackson*), Pamela Keller (*Jackie Lee French*), Gordon Hurst (*Monroe*), Mike Hosford (*Johnny*), Faye Jordan (*nurse*), Charlie Seybert (*Andy Fanner*), Grover Lewis (*Mr Crawford*), Rebecca Ulrick (*Marlene*), Merrill Shepherd (*Agnes*), Buddy Wood (*Bud*), Kenny Wood (*Ken*), Leon Brown (*cowboy in café*), Bobby McGriff (*truck driver*), Jack Mueller (*oil pumper*), Robert Arnold (*Brother Blanton*), Frank Marshall (*Tommy Logan*), Otis Elmore (*first mechanic*), Charles Salmon (*roughneck driver*), George Gaulden (*cowboy*), Will Morris Hannis (*gas station man*), and the Leon Miller Band.

1951. In Anarene, a small, dust-laden, one-horse town in Texas (1), there are few distractions for the local youth apart from their sexual exploits and the weekly picture show. Sonny Crawford – having broken with his bovine, steady girlfriend Charlene, and though envious of his friend Duane (2), who seems to have found favour with the local belle Jacy – drifts into a liaison with Ruth (3), the neglected wife of the football coach.

Jacy has higher aspirations than Duane and leaves him at the local Christmas dance to attend a much smarter, nude swimming party where she attracts the attention of Bobby Sheen, a rich,

2

5

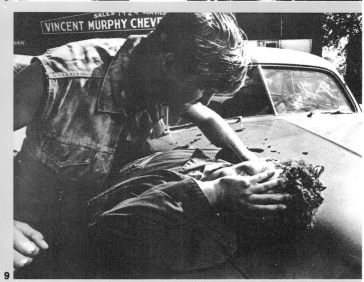

6

8

9

young playboy. To vent his frustration Duane, with Sonny, plays a cruel joke on Billy, a retarded boy, and is severely chastized by Sam the Lion (4), the cinema owner and Billy's protector. But Sam relents and on a fishing trip with Sonny reminisces (5) about how he once went swimming, naked, with a girl. Returning from a trip to Mexico with Duane, Sonny learns that Sam has suddenly died.

Sam's old flame was Lois Farrow, Jacy's mother, who now advises her daughter to lose her virginity (6). Jacy consents to go with Duane to a motel (7), mainly because Bobby Sheen has curtly told her he has no time for

virgins. It is an unsatisfactory session and Duane leaves town to enlist for Korea. Jacy learns of Bobby's imminent marriage and, out of pique, lures Sonny (8) away from Ruth. Duane returns and in the ensuing fight (9) Sonny's eye is badly hurt. Jacy is delighted to be the focal point of this row and coerces Sonny into eloping with her, making sure that her parents will find out in time and send her back to college.

Duane, due to leave for Korea, spends his last night in town with Sonny at the cinema's final show before it closes. Sonny sees Billy struck dead by a passing lorry and wretchedly returns to Ruth for consolation (10).

10

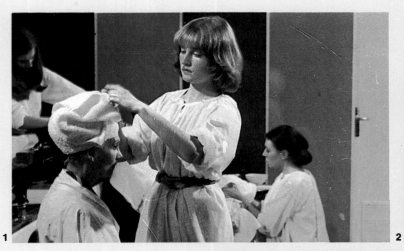

Claude Goretta's *The Lacemaker* follows the tenets of the British Free Cinema movement of the Fifties with which the director was closely associated. It is documentary-like in style, with unobtrusive camerawork, concentrating on the revealing details of behaviour in a methodical fashion that made the film seem slow to some critics. It expresses the social responsibilities of the artist, concerns itself with the dignity and well-being of ordinary people in society, and stresses the significance of everyday events.

In particular, *The Lacemaker* skilfully explores some divisive elements in civilized society that normally receive scant attention. The timid Pomme and the insecure François would seem well-suited to each other, but their relationship is not a balanced one. Pomme is only too anxious to please François, but he cannot resist dominating her and trying to change her. She is content with her humble job and her friendship with the shallow, extrovert Marylène. He wants her to improve herself to fit in with his circle of friends, and he drops her when the gap in their education and intellect seems to him too great.

Adding to this cultural divide is the social handicap of Pomme's working-class background, shown up on the visit to the country estate of François' well-off parents. François quickly changes the conversation when Pomme's line of work comes up and she – probably only because of nervousness – chokes on her food. Later, François' mother can only find in Pomme's favour that 'she seems very decent'.

After François ends the affair, another student accuses him of having treated Pomme like an employee whom he has then fired. Yet Pomme was happiest playing the role of servant – ironing François' clothes, cooking his food. In fact, *The Lacemaker* explores not only a sociological problem – the intolerance of the intelligent person towards the more simple-minded – but a psychological one peculiar to Pomme. Whereas Marylène externalizes her grief at the end of an affair and gets it out of her system, Pomme is shattered by the outcome of her first sexual relationship and withdraws into herself, succumbing to anorexia and mental breakdown.

THE LACEMAKER

Goretta subtly indicates some of the other reasons for Pomme's collapse. She has lacked a father and meant too much to her mother, who still thinks of her as a child. Pomme behaves in the immature way of a 13-year-old – scoffing food, looking for shells on a beach – and lacks social skills. She can neither swim nor dance and she retreats from groups. Marylène, though recognizing that Pomme is 'fragile', is ultimately more concerned with her own happiness, as is François who uses Pomme to bolster his own ego by sexual conquest.

François certainly makes Pomme happy, as is clear from her radiance on the beach the day after their first night together, but he will not accept lasting responsibility for her. It seems unreasonable to expect that he should, although Goretta argues: 'We are always responsible for somebody else, but we don't know it sometimes – that we are responsible for the other,' and seems to regard the problem as only one of incommunicability because Pomme and François have different ways of expressing themselves, rather than seeing them as ultimately incompatible.

Goretta puts his view in words at the end, quoting the Pascal Lainé novel on which the film is based:

'He came close to her, very close to her, but did not see her. Because she was one of those people who never reach out but who must be

patiently sought, whom one must know how to see. In bygone days, a painter would have chosen her for a genre painting. She would have been a seamstress, a water-bearer, or a lacemaker.'

Isabelle Huppert has said of her role:

'She's not a passive character really. She has a very strong interior life . . . you realize she feels within herself a passion, what a tragic heroine would feel, something really huge in herself, and you couldn't see it.'

Perhaps this gulf between inner feelings and actions indicates a sickness rather than hidden depth of character. . . . Certain shots of

Pomme suggest a blankness, a lack of inner feelings, a need for outside stimuli to bring her to life.

At any rate, Pomme's final prolonged stare into the camera – as though posing for a portrait by Vermeer, one of whose paintings of working-women gives the film its title – invites each spectator to look beyond external appearances and to judge how they would have responded to her. It certainly seems true that Pomme would have been happier in a less complicated age. Her condition is both tragic and moving, whether or not society and François can be held responsible for the causes leading to her final breakdown.   ALLEN EYLES

Directed by Claude Goretta, 1977

Prod co: Action Films/FR3 (Paris)/Citel Films (Geneva)/Filmproduktion Janus (Frankfurt). **exec prod:** Yves Peyrot. **prod:** Yves Gasser. **assoc prod:** Klaus Hellwig, Lise Fayolle. **sc:** Pascal Lainé, Claude Goretta, from the novel by Pascal Lainé. **photo** (Eastman Colour): Jean Boffety. **ed:** Joëlle van Effenterre, Nelly Meunier, Martine Charasson. **art dir:** Serge Etter, Claude Chevant. **mus:** Pierre Jansen. **sd:** Pierre Gamet, Bernard Chaumeil, Alex Pront, Claude Villand. **sd eff:** Jérôme Levy. **prod man:** Bernard Lorain. **ass dir:** Laurent Ferrier, Patrick Grandperret. **r/t:** 107 minutes. French title: *La Dentellière*. Released in GB as *The Lacemaker*.
Cast: Isabelle Huppert (*Béatrice, known as Pomme*), Yves Beneyton (*François Beligne*), Florence Giorgetti (*Marylène Thorent*), Anne Marie Düringer (*Pomme's mother*), Renata Schroeter (*Marianne*), Michel de Ré (*Gérard*), Jean Obé (*M. Beligne*), Monique Chaumette (*Mme Beligne*), Anne Deleuze, Rosine Rochette (*voices*).

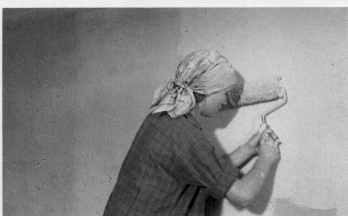

Pomme works as a trainee in a Paris hairdressing salon (1) and lives with her mother. Her friend Marylène helps them celebrate Pomme's 18th birthday. Pomme watches Marylène's emotional outburst when her protracted affair with a married man is terminated (2) and accompanies her on an end-of-season holiday in the Normandy seaside resort of Cabourg (3). Marylène moves in with an American she meets and leaves Pomme to her own devices.

Eating ice-cream, Pomme is befriended by a student, François. They become inseparable (4) and François tests her trust in him by having her close her eyes and follow his directions to the edge of a clifftop (5). He later presses her into sleeping with him.

Back in Paris she moves in with him and starts redecorating his flat (6), but feels out of place when a group of students hold a philosophical discussion (7). Introduced to François' parents, Pomme chokes on a fishbone and embarrasses her lover (8). At the flat, he grows unresponsive to her advances and later tells her they are not suited to each other (9).

She leaves him, becomes chronically ill and collapses in the street. Months later, François visits her in a sanatorium (10) and she tells him about an imaginary trip to Greece. He leaves, upset, and she resumes her knitting (11).

9

Where do you go when the record is over...

SATURDAY NIGHT FEVER

PARAMOUNT PICTURES PRESENTS
A ROBERT STIGWOOD PRODUCTION
JOHN TRAVOLTA KAREN GORNEY
"SATURDAY NIGHT FEVER"
Screenplay by NORMAN WEXLER
Directed by JOHN BADHAM

Disco was the first really new vernacular in popular music since the rock'n'roll of the late Fifties. Originally championed by blacks, high society and gays, the sub-culture mushroomed during the Seventies. In many ways it reflected and generated a new mood in the youth market – what author Tom Wolfe has described as 'The Me Generation'. Partly as a reaction against the Sixties' penchant for 'opting out' and partly as a practical response to an emerging recession, the Seventies saw a return to conservatism.

1

Pop commentator Nik Cohn noted this change in an article he wrote called *Tribal Rights of the New Saturday Night* which examined this new disco aesthetic. He concluded:

'The new generation takes few risks: it graduates, looks for a job, endures. And, once a week, on Saturday Night, it explodes.'

Although Cohn's article sparked off the idea for *Saturday Night Fever* the film shies away from any investigation of the real disco experience. Instead, director John Badham and producer Robert Stigwood took the popular notion of disco and used it both as a merchandising device and as a contemporary context for the film's age-old theme of growing up. Disco becomes a modern emblem for the kind of confused and alienated youth that has been in currency since James Dean. It is a retreat from the demands and hypocrisy of real life. Tony Manero escapes to the 2001 Odyssey disco where he can find respect away from his family and his tedious job. His parents, second generation Italians who inhabit an ethnic ghetto of Brooklyn, have always compared him unfavourably with his elder brother Frank, who is preparing for priesthood. And the only satisfaction that his job offers is the money to subsidise the Saturday night ritual. His athletic dancing has made him into a neighbourhood hero with the result that when he enters the club the crowd parts like the Red Sea.

But the film suggests that disco represents a cacophony of machismo, racism, tunnel vision, narcissism, aimlessness and cruelty. It underlines this again and again through a bumper bundle of relentlessly exaggerated imagery and sub-plots.

Tony prepares for the evening's entertainment in a bedroom plastered with posters of popular icons like Farrah Fawcett-Majors, Bruce Lee, Al Pacino and Sylvester Stallone. The camera lingers over every detail of Tony's obsessive preparation: from body cologne to jet-black briefs, amulets, a gold crucifix, platform shoes, patterned shirt, dapper suit and endless hair

4

disco mentality has been ladled down the audience's throats, the film proceeds to show how Tony transcends it through a series of stagey and unconvincing incidents. The most climactic shock is the dance contest in which Tony is partnering Stephanie. Up until then, any possibility of Tony furthering himself has revolved around disco. When the long-awaited final actually happens, it lands two unexpected punches. Tony discovers not only Real Emotion for Stephanie but also Moral Outrage when he becomes convinced that their winning of the first prize is the rigged result of ethnic jealousy. Despite giving an infinitely superior performance, a Puerto Rican couple have to be content with second place, and a horrified Tony gives them his prize.

Saturday Night Fever had an explosive effect. In many respects the phenomenon became more important than the film. Stigwood's merchandising assault was a test case in combining military precision with extravagant gambling in both the selling and the promotion of the film.

Its massive box-office success encouraged a rash of disco-related projects like *Thank God It's Friday*, *The Stud* (both 1978), *American Gigolo* (1980) and even *Looking for Mr Goodbar* (1977). And it launched the career of John Travolta whose pin-up appeal had already been proved in the American television

Directed by John Badham, 1977

Prod co: Paramount. **exec prod:** Kevin McCormick. **prod:** Robert Stigwood. **assoc prod:** Milt Felsen. **prod co-ordinator:** Arlene Albertson. **sc:** Norman Wexler, from the story by Nik Cohn. **photo** (Movielab): Ralf D. Bode. **ed:** David Rawlins. **des:** Charles Bailey, George Detitta. **cost:** Patrizia von Brandenstein. **chor:** Lester Wilson, Jo-Jo Smith. **mus:** The Bee Gees, Yvonne Elliman, Tavares, David Shire, MFSB, Walter Murphy, The Trammps, Kool and the Gang, Rick Dees, K. C. and the Sunshine Band. **sd:** Michael Colgan, Les Lazarowitz, John K. Wilkinson, Robert W. Glass Jr, John T. Reitz. **tech con:** James Gambina. **stunt co-ordinator:** Paul Nuckles. **ass dir:** Allan Wertheim, Joseph Ray. **prod man:** John Nicolella. **r/t:** 119 mins.

Cast: John Travolta (*Tony Manero*), Karen Lynn Gorney (*Stephanie*), Barry Miller (*Bobby C*), Joseph Cali (*Joey*), Paul Pape (*Double J*), Donna Pescow (*Annette*), Bruce Ornstein (*Gus*), Julie Bovasso (*Flo*), Martin Shakar (*Frank Manero Jr*), Val Bisoglio (*Frank Manero Sr*), Monti Rock III (*DJ*), Sam J. Coppola (*Fusco*), Nina Hansen (*grandmother*), Lisa Peluso (*Linda*), Denny Dillon (*Doreen*), Bert Michaels (*Pete*), Robert Costanza (*paint store customer*), Robert Weil (*Becker*), Shelly Blatt (*girl in disco*), Fran Drescher (*Connie*), Donald Gantry (*Jay Langhart*), Murray Moston (*haberdashery salesman*), William Andrews (*detective*), Ann Travolta (*pizza girl*), Helen Travolta (*lady in paint store*), Ellen March (*bartender*).

Tony Manero only comes alive on Saturday nights at the 2001 Odyssey disco. It is his escape from a boring job in a hardware store (1), and a bickering family who live in Brooklyn (2). The disco announces a dance contest and Tony reluctantly agrees to partner the long-suffering Annette (3). However he drops her for new arrival Stephanie (4), who derides his lack of ambition and boasts about her own rising social status.

Tony is waylaid by problems with his gang (5) who get involved in a violent fight with a rival Puerto Rican gang; they then attack some Puerto Ricans only to discover later that they might have picked on the wrong 'spics'.

Back at the disco, Tony and Stephanie win the competition (6) but Tony, convinced that the result is rigged against a superior Puerto Rican couple (7), who come second, hands them the first prize.

In his frustration, he makes brutish approaches to Stephanie who runs away. Tony rejoins his coterie and they gang-rape Annette in the car. They drive to their favourite bridge from which the hysterical Bobby plunges to his death. This is too much for an already disillusioned Tony, and he travels aimlessly around on the subway (8). He finally confronts Stephanie, tells her of his decision to leave Brooklyn and the two finish as friends.

71

THE WHO PRESENTS THE MOVIE
QUADROPHENIA
A WAY OF LIFE!

QUADROPHENIA

THE WHO FILMS Present A CURBISHLEY BAIRD PRODUCTION QUADROPHENIA
Musical Directors ROGER DALTREY • JOHN ENTWISTLE • PETE TOWNSHEND
Screenplay by DAVE HUMPHRIES • MARTIN STELLMAN • FRANC RODDAM • Produced by ROY BAIRD & BILL CURBISHLEY
Directed by FRANC RODDAM • A POLYTEL FILM • [DOLBY STEREO]

R RESTRICTED

RELEASED BY WORLD NORTHAL CORPORATION

It was no coincidence that *Quadrophenia* was made in the slipstream of the punk revolution in Britain, or that two of its stars – Sting, the lead singer of the Police, and Toyah Willcox – were, if not punks, prominent 'New Wave' personalities. Punk not only regenerated rock music, it invaded the film industry as well – resulting in some excellent British movies, including *Jubilee* (1978), *Rude Boy*, *The Great Rock'n'Roll Swindle* and *Breaking Glass* (all 1980). *Quadrophenia* is the best – pumped high with the adrenalin of the late Seventies but a celebration of the kindred teenage energy and excitement of the mod era of the mid-Sixties.

Significantly, when director Franc Roddam first discussed the film with Pete Townshend, the leader of The Who whose album *Quadrophenia* is based on, their talk was of punk, not just as a musical movement but as something that they thought was going to influence fashion, 'architecture, design, all sorts of things', and possibly day-to-day life most of all. If the adornments adopted by kids of 1976 and after –

plastic, rubber, swastikas, bondage – are aesthetically different from the parkas, tailored suits, scooters and 'blues' of 1964, their sociological import is the same; it's just that one is a revolt into style, the other a revolt into anarchy. Living a lifestyle is what *Quadrophenia* is all about, and living it to the full; it doesn't matter who you are – a Ted, a mod, a rocker, a punk or post-punk – the search for identity is universal.

Accordingly Jimmy and his mates wear parkas, mohair suits and Staprest Levis; ride Vespas and Lambrettas; crash a straight party and put The Who's 'My Generation' on the record player; grope with girls dressed in leather macs; puke up in the gents; smash the car of a spiv who sells them dud blues; and break into a chemist's to get the real thing – which they scoff like sweets. Being young though has its attendant problems, especially if, like Jimmy, you are 'quadrophenic' – suffering from a sort of double schizophrenia, a fact reflected in the mirrors on his scooter – which, as the film's publicity suggests, is 'a

condition of today'. Jimmy has to cope with his boring job, his unsympathetic parents and the aloofness of Steph. He experiences guilt when his mates beat up his old schoolfriend who happens to have a leather jacket and a motorcycle; and he knows all the cold, damp loneliness of masturbating himself to sleep in his seedy bedroom.

Even in Brighton on the longed for day of mod-rocker confrontation, Jimmy is a hurt and alienated figure, watching the icy, silver shore at dawn. But his volatile state of mind and the constant intake of blues means that lows are quickly followed by highs. Next comes the ultimate high: the march of the mods along the prom, the bloody running battle with the rockers and the escape up a back alleyway where Jimmy and Steph finally make love. Even being arrested is okay when the Ace Face shares the same Black Maria.

Then comes the backlash. For Jimmy, Brighton and the mod life must continue, but up in the city disillusion rapidly sets in. Steph, cold and logical, has gone off with his best friend and the gang has already forgotten Brighton. When his scooter is 'killed' by a mail van, Jimmy effectively loses his identity too, and – 'out of his brain on the train', his eyes shadowed with the darkness growing in him – heads off for Brighton, now bleak and sordid.

With the demise of the Ace Face, Jimmy steals his scooter and apparently rides it over a cliff, committing a real rock'n'roll suicide. Or does he? The film's opening shot is of the lone mod walking back from the edge as Roger Daltrey of The Who screams 'Can you see the real me?' on the soundtrack. It may be a harsh judgment, but at the end Jimmy too has copped out, and is forced to accept the real world in

which pop music, youth and love are as ephemeral as each wave that breaks on Brighton beach.

Quadrophenia, then, is a rock dream, enjoyable while it lasts but fired with the knowledge that being a fervent mod – or whatever – is not enough. Pete Townshend surely understands this as does Phil Daniels, whose portrayal of Jimmy is immaculate:

'I had a really interesting talk to Roger Daltrey one day on the beach in Brighton. He's sayin' there's a Jimmy in all of us, we're all Jimmy in a way . . . so that's how I try to play it, like a typical kid.'

Roddam understands it too and if *Quadrophenia* is finally a tragic evocation of teenage wasteland, then at the same time its images of gleaming chrome scooters sparking through the London night are as magical a recommendation of being young as anything else that has been put on film.

GRAHAM FULLER

72

London, 1964. Jimmy and his friends Dave and Chalky are mods who spend their money on amphetamines, clothes and keeping their scooters on the road. At the public baths Jimmy meets Kevin, an old schoolfriend who is now a leather-jacketed rocker (1) and by rights an enemy. Jimmy gate-crashes a party where some of the mod girls – the aloof Steph (2) and the more amenable 'Monkey' – are dancing. Later, when one of the mods is attacked by rockers, his mates take revenge by severely beating up Kevin.

With the Battle of Brighton due to take place on the forthcoming bank holiday, Jimmy tries to get some pills but is swindled by a crooked dealer (3) – so the boys smash up his car. They finally get their drugs by burgling a chemist's and set off for Brighton. The mods – led by the elegant Ace Face (4) – gather on the sea-front and

Jimmy renews his pursuit of Steph. At a dance he steals the glory from Ace by leaping from the balcony onto the crowded dance floor, but is then thrown out. A night on the beach is followed by a bloody battle with the rockers (5). Diverted up an alley, Jimmy and Steph make love (6) but Jimmy, with Ace, is arrested on rejoining the fight. He is fined in court and returns to London. His mother throws him out of the house and he quits his job in the mail-room of an advertising agency. When he finds that Steph is now Dave's girl he starts a fight and his mates turn against him. A little later he crashes his scooter (7).

Fortified with blues and drink he goes back to Brighton on the 5.15 train (8), but, horrified to see that Ace is a servile hotel bellboy (9) steals his scooter, drives it up to the cliffs (10) and over the edge into the sea.

Directed by Franc Roddam, 1979
Prod co: The Who Films, A Polytel Film. **exec prod:** Roger Daltrey, John Entwistle, Pete Townshend, Keith Moon, David Gideon Thomson. **prod:** Roy Baird, Bill Curbishley. **assoc prod:** John Peverall. **sc:** Dave Humphries, Martin Stellman, Franc Roddam, Alan Fletcher, Pete Townshend, Chris Stamp. **photo** (Eastman Colour): Brian Tufano. **ed:** Sean Barton, Mike Taylor. **prod des:** Simon Holland. **ass art dir:** Andrew Sanders. **set dec:** Ken Wheatley. **cost:** Joyce Stoneman. **mus dir:** Mike Shaw, Roger Daltrey, John Entwistle, Pete Townshend. **mus:** Cross Section, The Who, Zoot Money, The High Numbers, The Merseybeats, Derrick Morgan, James Brown, The Ronettes, The Crystals, The Orlons, The Cascades, The Supremes, Marvin Gaye, The Chiffons, The Kingsmen, Manfred Mann, Booker T & the MGs. **sd:** John Ireland, Christian Wrangler, Bill Rowe. **ass dir:** Ray Corbett. **prod ass:** Caroline Hagen. **r/t:** 120 mins.
Cast: Phil Daniels (*Jimmy*), Leslie Ash (*Steph*), Philip Davis (*Chalky*), Mark Wingett (*Dave*), Sting (*Ace Face*), Raymond Winstone (*Kevin*), Garry Cooper (*Peter*), Gary Shail (*Spider*), Toyah Willcox (*Monkey*), Trevor Laird (*Ferdy*), Kate Williams (*Jimmy's mother*), Michael Elphick (*Jimmy's father*), Kim Neve (*Yvonne*), Benjamin Whitrow (*Mr Fulford*), Daniel Peacock (*Danny*), Jeremy Child (*agency man*), John Phillips (*magistrate*), Timothy Spall (*projectionist*), Olivier Pierre (*tailor*), George Innes (*café owner*), John Bindon (*Harry*), P.H. Moriarty (*barman at villain's pub*), Hugh Lloyd (*Mr Cale*).

THESE ARE THE ARMIES OF THE NIGHT.
They are 100,000 strong. They outnumber the cops five to one.
They could run New York City. Tonight they're all out to get the Warriors.

Paramount Pictures Presents A Lawrence Gordon Production "THE WARRIORS"
Executive Producer Frank Marshall Based Upon the Novel by Sol Yurick
Screenplay by David Shaber and Walter Hill Produced by Lawrence Gordon
Directed by Walter Hill Read the Dell Book

Directed by Walter Hill, 1979
Prod co: Paramount. **exec prod:** Frank Marshall. **prod:** Lawrence Gordon. **assoc prod:** Joel Silver. **sc:** David Shaber, Walter Hill, from the novel by Sol Yurick. **photo** (Movielab): Andrew Laszlo. **sp eff:** Edward Drohan. **ed:** David Holden. **art dir:** Don Swanagan, Bob Wightman, Fred Weiler. **cost:** Bobbie Mannix, Mary Ellen Winston. **mus:** Barry De Vorzon, Kenny Vance, Joe Ferla, Rob Mounsey, Paul Griffin. **songs:** Joe Walsh, Arnold McCuller, Frederick LaPlano, Mandrill, Genya Raven, Johnny Vastano, Desmond Child, Rouge, The Mersh Brothers. **sd:** Jack Jacobsen, Al Mian, Tex Rudloff, Don Mitchell, Richard Cline. **sd eff:** Howard Beals, George Watters II, Allan Murray, William Andrews, Lee Osborne. **ass dir:** David O. Sosna. **prod man:** John Starke. **prod co-ord:** Gail Geibel. **r/t:** 94 mins.
Cast: Michael Beck (*Swan*), James Remar (*Ajax*), Thomas Waites (*Fox*), Dorsey Wright (*Cleon*), Brian Tyler (*Snow*), David Harris (*Cochise*), Tom McKitterick (*Cowboy*), Marcelino Sanchez (*Rembrandt*), Terry Michos (*Vermin*), Deborah Van Valkenburgh (*Mercy*), Roger Hill (*Cyrus*), David Patrick Kelly (*Luther*), Lynne Thigpen (*DJ*), Ginny Ortiz (*candy store girl*), Mercedes Ruehl (*policewoman*), John Snyder (*gas station man*), Dennis Gregory (*Masai*), Gwynn Press, Jodi Price, Jeffrey Scott, Carl Brown (*prom couples*).

After the Battle of Cunaxa, not far from Babylon, in September 401 BC, the Greek prince Cyrus lay dead after a failed attempt to gain the throne, and 10,000 Greeks were faced with surrender to an alien king or a long march home. Xenophon, a young Athenian, led them back through 1000 miles of hostile territory, hounded by barbarians.

Such is the outline of Xenophon's *Anabasis* – literally, 'The journey up' – on which Sol Yurick based his novel *The Warriors*, translating the Greek mercenaries into a modern New York street gang desperately engaged in the tale's ambiguous kind of warfare. They are running for their home turf while fighting a rearguard action against all the other gangs whose territory they must cross – it is not exactly a retreat, but neither is it the kind of confrontation that the epic usually glorified. In Yurick's novel, grounded in a solid social-realist context, Cyrus' conclave in the Bronx breaks up due to generalized gang frictions, and the Warriors have trouble getting back to Coney Island because they misread the subway maps! Their exploits *en route* include stabbing a passer-by for fun and the subsequent gang-bang of a passing girl to subdue their excitement over the murder. Their return is no triumph, but just another round of deprivation and welfare cheques.

Walter Hill's movie bears virtually no resemblance to the novel other than the basic framework of the run home. It opens with a long shot of the Coney Island ferris wheel – its name, 'Wonder Wheel', illuminated brightly against the deep black of the night; then overhead shots of the snaking subway trains in electric colours, their noise subdued by electronic music on the soundtrack. It is clear from the start that the movie is a kind of neon fantasy; a stylized dance through a subterranean city of the imagination.

On the rare occasions that the Warriors surface onto ground level, the streets are depopulated of 'civilian' life. The Orphans, a bunch of dispirited 'wimps', are sent scurrying by Swan's petrol-bombing of a nearby car – to which there is no local response. A diversionary fire, set up to delay the Warriors, is fought by unseen firemen. Indeed, any signs of 'civilian' life are treacherously camouflaged. Ajax succumbs to the siren voice of a temptress in the park only to be handcuffed to the bench – she is an undercover cop. A group of women who entice three of the gang up to street level from the Union Square subway turn out to be the Lizzies – a lesbian gang of lethal intention, if less than effective action. The night-time people rule and the streets of New York are emptied of everyday life.

All of which serves to highlight the film's one confrontation between the gang and 'straight' people. Some fancily dressed late-night revellers board the subway and sit opposite Swan and his girl Mercy. They all stare at each other with the blank incomprehension of aliens. Mercy raises her hand to adjust her dishevelled hair, and Swan without a word or even a glance at her, restrains her hand in mid-flight. With an understatement typical of his films, Hill compresses volumes of social and psychological comment into the briefest cinematic gesture.

The film's only other concession toward social background comes when the gang finally make it back to Coney Island as dawn is breaking over the silent, rainswept funfair; the 'Wonder Wheel' no longer looks so very wonderful. 'This is what we fought all night to get back to!' says one of the gang. After that the face-off on the beach with Luther and the Rogues is almost perfunctory. Clearly, what interests Hill is the race itself, not the prize.

The absolutes of winning and losing are central to all of Hill's films, but the main concern is centred on the grace of the sport itself. As in *The Getaway* (1972) – a film he scripted for director Sam Peckinpah – and *The Driver* (1978), survival is all and the contender most likely to attain it is the one who engages in the struggle with the most commitment and expertise.

Rarely has the expertise of violent combat been so gracefully composed as in *The Warriors*. When they take on the Baseball Furies in the darkened park, Ajax's threat – 'I'm going to shove that bat up your ass and turn you into a popsicle' – is duly realized in a sequence which combines all the energy of a Kung Fu movie with the controlled precision and style of modern dance movement. The rumble in a subway washroom with the Punks, a gang wearing pre-teenagers' dungarees and roller-skates, is similarly orchestrated.

If, finally, the audience is left with the sneaking suspicion that the well-fed, photogenic Warriors have as much street-credibility as the gangs in *West Side Story* (1961), there is at least the consolation that they are far better choreographed.

CHRIS PEACHMENT

The Warriors, a street gang from Coney Island (1), converge with all the other gangs in New York on a conclave held in the Bronx by Cyrus (2), a black leader who dreams of uniting the gangs into a force that will control the city.

Cyrus is shot by Luther, the psychotic leader of the Rogues, and the meeting is broken up by police. In the ensuing mêlée the Warriors are blamed for the shooting. They are pursued by other gangs but make it to the subway at 96th Street.

Due to a fire they are forced to surface onto the street where they encounter the Orphans. The Warriors thrash them but as they return to the subway find they have acquired Mercy, the Orphans' leader's girl, as a companion.

Separated from the rest of the gang by police, Swan the leader, Ajax his lieutenant and two other Warriors beat up the Baseball Furies (3) in a park but Ajax is then arrested by a plain-clothes policewoman. Three other Warriors are enticed by the Lizzies, a lesbian gang, back to their headquarters (4) and narrowly escape being wiped out. The reunion of the Warriors in Union Square leads to another battle in a men's washroom with the Punks (5). The Warriors and Mercy (6) finally make it back as dawn breaks over Coney Island (7), and emerge to find Luther and the Rogues coming for them. In the final showdown on the beach (8), Luther pulls a gun but Swan throws his switchblade into Luther's wrist.

Little Darlings

They may be smart, precocious, cheeky, appealing or even appalling; they may have famous parents or come from 'nowhere'; they may go on to greater things or disappear from the public gaze forever. They are today's child stars

Until the mid-Fifties, the major child performers in Hollywood and Britain embodied a basic innocence. However, former juvenile star Natalie Wood's brilliant portrait of troubled adolescence in *Rebel Without a Cause* (1955) heralded a transition from innocence to experience among screen youngsters over the next five years. America dominated this territory, with Elvis Presley in the vanguard. Britain, at the decade's end, could only offer Cliff Richard as a pale reply.

At the beginning of the Sixties, however, the balance unexpectedly shifted. Only a few American children made their mark. Patty Duke, as the deaf-and-dumb Helen Keller in *The Miracle Worker* (1962), achieved a *tour de force* of grimacing, madly wilful pathos, combining rage and helplessness with happiness, charm and shy, silent love. Tippy Walker and Merri Spaeth in *The World of Henry Orient* (1964)

provided a fresh depiction of adolescent friendship: their first meeting, when they exchange trivial personal details in Central Park, establishes a spontaneous flavour and a later conversation allows Spaeth's homely, pensive face some touching reactions.

Sugar and spice . . .
But it was from Britain, where the Swinging Sixties were soon to erupt, that the pioneering young star of the era came. Hayley Mills made her debut as the witness to crime in *Tiger Bay* (1959) and in Walt Disney's 1960 remake of the old Mary Pickford vehicle *Pollyanna*, she exhibited absolute informality and lack of sentimentality, as well as a genuine comic sense. Back in Britain for the whimsical religious fable *Whistle Down the Wind* (1961), she found herself upstaged by a highly amusing, hoarsely stammering, beadily suspicious little

boy named Alan Barnes. However, reunited with Disney for *The Parent Trap* (1961), when she played twin sisters, she was permitted far greater freedom of expression. Her mannerisms seemed legitimate and neatly calculated rather than synthetic or obtrusive: the wrinkling of forehead, eyes and nose; the eagerly thoughtfully licking lips and tongue; the fingers unconsciously, meditatively pulling at lapel; the mischievous or disconcerted little cough; the eloquently rolling eyes; the suddenly convulsive, squawking tantrums and ghoulish mugging for humorous effect.

In a later Disney picture, *Summer Magic* (1963), she tasted the dreams, joys and pangs of youthful romance; her appealing histrionic tricks and quirks were toned down and replaced by a relaxed and restrained confidence. Admittedly confidence was not quite enough for total success in a more ambitious, tragicomic role in *The Chalk Garden* (1964). Nevertheless, her soliloquy of would-be-maternal and lonely tenderness to a doll emerged as the movie's single fully realized episode. During the rest of the Sixties, Hayley Mills rang other agreeable changes on adolescent pleasure and pain in films like the romantic romp *The Truth About Spring* (1965) and the wry north country comedy *The Family Way* (1966). But gradually her vehicles became less satisfactory. Pieces such as the tiresome 1967 film of the Noel Coward story *Pretty Polly*, and the distasteful shocker *Twisted Nerve* (1968), did her little good; and the uneasy screen version

f Kingsley Amis' *Take a Girl Like You* (1969)
oreshadowed the decline of her promise.

Girls will be girls

n retrospect Hayley Mills' personality and
talent appeared more at home in the old
traditions of pert wholesomeness than in the
tough, knowing new Sixties trend for youthful
sophistication. In contrast, another notable
young British actress, Pamela Franklin, pro-
gressed from her part as the eerie child in *The
Innocents* (1961) – an adaptation of Henry
James' story *The Turn of the Screw* – to a vivid
portrayal of tomboyishness in the big-game-
hunting adventure *The Lion* (1962), and an
even more telling sketch of flirtatiousness in
the thriller *The Nanny* (1965). In a melodrama
about orphans, *Our Mother's House* (1967), she
admirably conveys a girl's quasi-incestuous
desire for her supposed father, and if the weird
crime tale *The Night of the Following Day* (1968)
requires her merely to sob and/or scream, she
seized a much richer opportunity in the film of
Muriel Spark's idiosyncratic school yarn *The
Prime of Miss Jean Brodie* (1969). As a provocat-
ive pupil, she adopts an impassively enigmatic
facial and vocal technique, leaving the exact
degree of virtue and vice in her character an
ambiguity. Apart from a striking performance
as a medium in the paranormal extravaganza
The Legend of Hell House (1973), most of her
subsequent work has been for American TV.

Far left: Ryan and Tatum O'Neal in Paper
Moon. *Above left: Helen Keller (Patty Duke)
and her teacher (Anne Bancroft) in* The
Miracle Worker. *Above: Hayley Mills as a
child getting the better of her abductor (Horst
Buchholz) in* Tiger Bay. *Below right: Elizabeth
(Jane Asher, left) catches a thief in* The
Greengage Summer. *Below left: the governess
and her charge (Deborah Kerr and Pamela
Franklin) in* The Innocents

After a faintly sententious early role in the
emotional drama *The Greengage Summer*
(1961), Jane Asher developed swiftly in the
Edgar Allan Poe fantasy *The Masque of the Red
Death* (1964), but attained her peak at the start
of a new decade in *Deep End* (1970), the Polish
director Jerzy Skolimowski's extraordinary depiction of sleazy London. In one sequence she
brought ferocious conviction to a superbly
contemptuous, hysterical monologue ending
in the dismissal of her older, married lover (not
surprisingly, perhaps – for the scene was
written by her). During the Seventies, however, Asher gravitated increasingly towards
television and theatre.

A calm in Britain

The remainder of Britain's youthful acting
record is distinctly fragmentary. A powerful
version of William Golding's allegory of child
castaways, *Lord of the Flies* (1963), featured a
remarkable vignette from Hugh Edwards as
Piggy, the prim, pompous, yet endearing 'fat
boy' who is the tragic butt of bullies. In another
distinguished literary transposition, an adaptation of Richard Hughes' *A High Wind in
Jamaica* (1965), Deborah Baxter persuasively
suggested a teenager's capacity to ensnare a
pirate chief.

The Seventies spectacularly accelerated the
Sixties tendency towards street-wise adolescence in the cinema, besides restoring the U.S.
to supremacy in that field. True, there was a
handful of noteworthy British newcomers:
Dominic Guard was vulnerable yet dogged as
the boy enmeshed in adult traumas in *The Go-
Between* (1971); and a more lasting impression
was made by Jenny Agutter, who matured
from the delightful period family saga *The
Railway Children* (1970) and the grimmer Australian parable *Walkabout* (1971), to grown-up
stardom in movies like the elaborate psychiat-
ric study *Equus* (1977).

Near the decade's end Toyah Wilcox –
following a graphic cameo as the heartless
tease in George Cukor's television version of
The Corn is Green (1978) – turned to the big
screen in Derek Jarman's punk epic *Jubilee*
(1978) and unconventional *The Tempest* (1979).

Yet the lion's share of juvenile talent has
come from the United States. Cukor directed
one of these new hopefuls, Cindy Williams, in
Travels With My Aunt (1972), a beguiling and

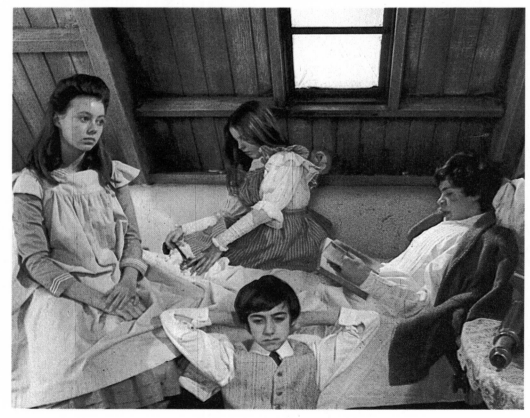

underpraised adaptation of Graham Greene
serio-comic novel in which she plays a hipp
sharing a brief, witty, yet affecting sem
platonic rapport with a staid Englishma
Williams moved on to appear as the touchin
rather drab 'steady' girlfriend of a stud
American Graffiti (1973), the nostalgic chro
icle of Sixties teenage morals, and as th
nervily guilt-ridden lover spied on in *T*
Conversation (1974). Since then she has four
her greatest public as Shirley in th
American television series *Laverne and Shirle*

Ugly ducklings . . .

In the same year as *American Graffiti* a mo
sensational stir was generated by a very youn
performer. In Peter Bogdanovich's Depression
era comedy *Paper Moon*, nine-year-old Tatu
O'Neal shared a splendidly funny fathe
daughter relationship with her real-life da
Ryan – creating a faultless rendering of bratt
surly, foul-mouthed, yet winning childishnes
unmarred by any strenuously coy pseude
refinement. When she lights a cigarette, i
hales, blows the smoke out and gazes di
enchantedly at her outraged pa, she looks
battle-scarred, bored adult – but also the k
she actually is. When her po-faced hostilit
abruptly melts into a dawning, hal
suppressed grin, coupled with a quick, sidelor
glance at her 'poppa' – or when she turns on
full-strength beam of infantile delight – he
appeal is irresistible.

Added to this, her delivery of scornfu
implacable one-liners is flawless: witness th
moment at the fun-fair when her father asser
that he possesses scruples, she withering
retorts 'Whatever they are, I bet they don
belong to you'. Largely retaining her freshne
in the baseball jape *The Bad News Bears*, an
the homage to silent movies *Nickelodeon* (bot
1976), O'Neal found the upper-middle-clas
English horse-training atmosphere of *Inte
national Velvet* (1978) less congenial, and ofte
lapsed into arch ecstasy or schmaltz
melancholy.

. . . and budding swans

The teenage sex-satire *Little Darlings* (1980
saw her out-acted by a newcomer from TV

*Top left: watchful Piggy (Hugh Edwards) and
Ralph (James Aubrey) in* Lord of the Flies. *To
right: Toyah Willcox as Miranda in* The
Tempest. *Above left: a note passes between Le*
(Dominic Guard) and Marion (Julie Christie) i
The Go-Between. *Left: Bobbie (Jenny Agutter*
*Phyllis (Sally Thomsett) and Peter (Gary
Warren) worry about their Russian refugee
(Gordon Whiting) in* The Railway Children

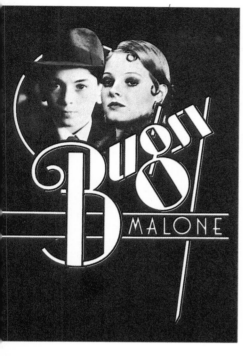

Above: Scott Baio and Jodie Foster star in Alan Parker's gangster spoof. Above right: possessed by the devil – Linda Blair in The Exorcist. *Above, far right: Linda Manz as a girl who leaves Chicago for the wide open spaces in* Days of Heaven. *Right: father and son (Jon Voight and Ricky Schroder) look for 'mum' in the crowd in* The Champ, *and (below right) father and son (Dustin Hoffman and Justin Henry) think about her in* Kramer vs Kramer

the abrasive but moving Kristy McNichol. In one sequence – where she confesses the loss of her virginity – McNichol poignantly communicates the character's momentary inability to be truthful, tears starting to her eyes as her face works in tremulous smiles, her head turning away for an instant as she steels herself to the revelation.

With her mixture of street-smart poise and underlying sensitivity, Kristy McNichol resembles Jodie Foster, who surely remains the strongest prospect of the crop of Seventies' children, and fully demonstrated her powers in *Echoes of a Summer* (1975) and *The Little Girl who Lives Down the Lane* (1977). In the former, as an eleven-year-old doomed to die of a heart ailment, she is stoically witty and piercingly sad, as captured in her nocturnal venture with her father; her sardonic gags and Southern drawl in a discussion with her doctor; her fierce rejection of her stern governess' Christian faith; her scenes with a young male chum, in which she makes him hold her hand as an emblem of the sexual fulfilment she is never to have; and the sequence where she plies her mother with queries about adult life and love, then voices the longing to be twenty-five for a day and have 'a secret date with a married man'. She was even more unerring as *The Little Girl Who Lives Down the Lane*, whether in her cautiously budding amorous harmony with a lame youth, or in her glacial disclosures of her deathly past.

Earlier she had etched a cherishable vignette in *Alice Doesn't Live Here Anymore* (1974) and then came *Taxi Driver* (1976), where as a juvenile whore she achieves a bitter-sweet sense of the character re-awakening to her untainted self, laughing to hide her hurt when

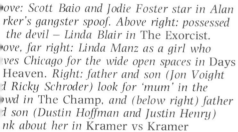

79

the cabbie reveals that her 'ponce' has cruelly termed her a 'piece of chicken'. And as a gangster's moll in *Bugsy Malone* (1976), she delivers cracks like 'Why don't you smear my lipstick a little?' with utter aplomb.

By comparison, Foster's next two Disney pictures were bound to be anti-climactic. *Freaky Friday* (1976) sees her as a girl who magically assumes her mother's brain, and Foster marvellously transmits – by use of facial expression and vocal intonation – her jealous appraisal of a predatory female secretary. In *Candleshoe* (1977), as a delinquent with a conscience, she is touchingly brusque – 'I'm no good at goodbyes', she says to the old lady played by Helen Hayes. Foster's two most recent movies, *Foxes* and *Carny* (both 1980), signal the next phase of a potentially fruitful career.

Among the other transatlantic juveniles of the Seventies, the principal girls include Linda Blair, the diabolically possessed victim in *The Exorcist* (1973); Linda Manz, throaty narrator of the farming epic *Days of Heaven* (1978); Quinn Cummings as the perky daughter in *The Goodbye Girl* (1977), and Lisa Lucas as a more serious daughter in *An Unmarried Woman* (1978); Diane Lane, one of the young lovers in *A Little Romance* (1979); and Brooke Shields, playing an adolescent prostitute in Louis Malle's stylish evocation of a New Orleans bordello, *Pretty Baby* (1978).

Enter the snails and puppydog tails!

Of the boys Jackie Earle Haley has singled himself out as the bizarre child in the Hollywood drama *Day of the Locust* (1975), and then in more orthodox roles in films such as *The Bad News Bears* and *Breaking Away* (1979); Justin Henry in the divorce drama *Kramer vs*

Above: an adolescent girl (Tatum O'Neal, righ at summer camp urges her friends to spy on the boys in Little Darlings. *Below: Brooke Shields and Susan Sarandon in* Pretty Baby

Kramer (1979); Ricky Schroder in the remak of the boxing soap-opera *The Champ* (1979) a the aristocratic weepie *Little Lord Fauntler* (1981); and Jeremy Levy as one of the mixed Rich Kids* (1979).

Levy's female co-star, Trini Alvarado, we on to appear in the teenage picture *Tim Square* (1980) with Robin Johnson, a ne comer of 15. Johnson goes further than ev Jodie Foster or Kristy McNichol in gru acerbic insurrection, perhaps only lacki their subtlety of emotion. All the same she clearly one of the great hopes for the future a as such warrants serious attention.

DOUGLAS McVA

Innocents abroad

The child star is a special breed, often exceptionally talented; most flower very early and only a few grow successfully into adult roles

The end of the Thirties and the beginning of World War II brought changes which affected the lives of millions of people. Even those distanced from the crunch of Hitler's boot were influenced by the reverberations it set up and the films of the day began to reflect a greater concern for realism and humanitarian values. Child stars were still popular but the candy-box appeal of Shirley Temple gave way to less sentimentalized embodiments of childish virtue, of whom the most successful and possibly the most talented was Margaret O'Brien (b.1937). Her old-fashioned dignity and emotional honesty seemed in keeping with the times and she scored an immediate success with her first starring role in *Journey for Margaret* (1942). MGM put her under contract and provided a number of parts over the next two years, in *Lost Angel, Jane Eyre* (both 1943), *Madame Curie* and *The Canterville Ghost* (both 1944). But it was not until *Meet Me in St Louis* (1944), in which she starred with Judy Garland, that she was able to display the full range of her talents, combining acting ability and showbiz razzmatazz to win a special Oscar. She later made *Music for Millions* (1944) and, with Edward G. Robinson, *Our Vines Have Tender Grapes* (1945) but then there was a shortage of good parts until her affecting portrayal of Beth, the sister who dies, in *Little Women* (1949).

The film which launched Margaret O'Brien's career, *Journey for Margaret*, told the story of a little girl evacuated to America at the time of the Blitz. In real life, war-time evacuation was bringing new child stars to Hollywood. Elizabeth Taylor (b.1932) arrived in 1940 and made a successful debut in *Lassie Come Home* (1943). MGM, encouraged by this and by the popularity of Margaret O'Brien, added her to their list of contract artists, putting her in *Jane Eyre* and *The White Cliffs of Dover* (1944). But it was her performance in *National Velvet* (1944), as the girl who dreams of winning the Grand National horse-race, that attracted critical attention and established her as a star.

Co-starring with Elizabeth Taylor in *Lassie Come Home* was another evacuee, Roddy McDowall (b.1928), who came with four years of film-acting experience behind him. His first Hollywood role was in John Ford's *How Green Was My Valley* (1941), a moving account of family life in a Welsh mining village, which won an Academy Award and brought its child star the certainty of more starring roles – in *The Pied Piper* (1942), *My Friend Flicka* (1943) and *Lassie Come Home*, for example.

Hollywood had its home-grown talent too: Dean Stockwell (b.1936) nearly stole the show from Gene Kelly and Frank Sinatra in *Anchors Aweigh* (1945) and his good looks and acting ability ensured a string of good parts in, for instance, Elia Kazan's *Gentleman's Agreement* (1947) and Joseph Losey's fantasy *The Boy With Green Hair* (1948), both of which dealt with racism. The success of Roddy McDowall and Dean Stockwell depended on their ability to convey both the strengths and the vulnerabilities of childhood, a mixture of qualities demonstrated to perfection in the dreamy devotion

of Brandon De Wilde (1942–72) as a boy who invests a gunfighter with heroic virtues in *Shane* (1953); De Wilde also re-created with memorable simplicity the role of John Henry in *The Member of the Wedding* (1952) which he had played on Broadway. The career of Bobby Driscoll (1937–1968) spanned the Forties and Fifties; he won a special Academy Award in 1949 as Outstanding Juvenile Actor and he was one of the first children to appear in Disney live-action features, notably *Treasure Island* (1950). Other notable child stars were

Above: Albert Lamorisse's Le Ballon Rouge (1956, The Red Balloon) was a delightful fantasy about a small boy (Pascal Lamorisse) and a balloon that follows him like a devoted pet

Natalie Wood (b.1938), who began at five with *Happy Land* (1943) but became established in *Miracle on 34th Street* (1947); and Peggy Ann Garner (b.1931) and Patty McCormack (b.1945), who made their marks in *A Tree Grows in Brooklyn* (1945) and *The Bad Seed* (1956) respectively.

Britain produced an armful of good young actors: John Howard Davies, Janette Scott, Bobby Henrey, Andrew Ray, Mandy Miller, Mark Lester and Jack Wild; but only Hayley Mills (b.1946) achieved any lasting success. Walt Disney put her under contract after seeing her in *Tiger Bay* (1959), playing a part originally intended for a boy, and gave her an Academy Award-winning role in *Pollyanna* (1960). After *Whistle Down the Wind* (1961), she was able to grow up through her films and continue as an adult star, a progression denied to most, with Elizabeth Taylor as one glittering exception. Adolescence brought to an end many a child's career, and although some pursued acting as a vocation it was mostly very much on the fringes of stardom.

The child star was a Hollywood phenomenon, the product of a system geared to the box-office and playing on the fantasy notions adults have of childhood, whatever the reality of their own experiences. Not everyone contributed to this adult conspiracy about childhood: *Captains Courageous* (1937) had illuminated for adults some aspects of growing up, and *Gentleman's Agreement* and *The Member of the Wedding* were resolutely unsentimental. It was not until the end of the war that children began to be used in a more meaningful and direct way. Vittorio De Sica took children from the streets, and extracted from them performances of outstanding clarity to make stringent comments on the exigencies of post-war Italian society in *Sciuscià* (1946, *Shoeshine*) and in his masterpiece *Ladri di Biciclette* (1948, *Bicycle Thieves*). Circumstances had ensured for these children a premature loss of innocence, a theme Carol Reed explored in *The Fallen Idol* (1948), scripted by Graham Greene, in which a young boy (Bobby Henrey) is overcome with fear and bewilderment when faced with the inexplicable passions of adults. In trying to protect the man he cares for, he unintentionally implicates his idol in murder.

The device of showing the adult world through the eyes of a child was developed with great force and imagination by René Clément in his anti-war film *Jeux Interdits* (1952, *Forbidden Games*). A little girl is adopted into a peasant family after she has seen her parents killed; she and the peasants' son begin to play out their fantasies about the death all around them by making a cemetery for dead animals. As their obsession grows, the fantasy world becomes their reality; and Clément's great achievement lies in his acceptance of children as they really are, intense, inconsistent, feeling creatures, retreating into fantasy when the adult world becomes too painful. In *The Go-Between* (1971) 13-year-old Leo (Dominic Guard) is unable to retreat and is instead pushed abruptly out of childhood when the puzzling events of a sensuous Edwardian summer, seen through his eyes, become crystallized in a glimpse of his previously admired friends (Alan Bates and Julie Christie) coupling in a stable. A more sentimentalized account of kids viewing the adult world was *Whistle Down the Wind*, in which a group of children believe a man they find sleeping in a barn to be Jesus; it lacked the knowledge of the essential truth about children that better films have demonstrated – that children are anarchists, primitive creatures with basic needs and desires, constantly rebelling against efforts to channel these forces according to standards acceptable to society.

François Truffaut, who was influenced by Jean Vigo and his view of rebellious youth in *Zéro de Conduite* (1933, *Nought for Behaviour*), understood

Top left: Roddy McDowall plays Huw Morgan, a boy who decides to leave the mining community, in How Green Was My Valley; the *Rhondda Valley setting more closely resembled an Irish country village. Top: Natalie Wood as the girl who believes she has met the real Father Christmas and Maureen O'Hara and John Payne in George Seaton's* Miracle on 34th Street. *Above: John Henry (Brandon De Wilde) the boy who dies, and Frankie (Julie Harris), the young girl who feels neglected by her family when her sister is getting married, in Fred Zinnemann's version of Carson McCullers' play* The Member of the Wedding

Above: Jane Wyman portrays the severe Aunt Polly, with Hayley Mills as her engaging niece in Pollyanna. *Above right: in* The Wild Child, *Victor, the wild boy of Aveyron, was played by Jean-Pierre Cargol, a young gipsy. Right: Alan Bates is a farmer involved in a secret love affair and Dominic Guard is his 'postman' in* The Go-Between. *Bottom: Harley Cokliss directs Ben Buckton in the role of a boy who befriends a spherical alien from outer space in* The Glitterball

this and his first important film, a short feature, *Les Mistons* (1957, *The Mischief Makers*) deals with a group of boys reacting noisily and defiantly when faced with the incomprehensible values of the adult world. Truffaut's championship of the bewildered adolescent pounding on the door of repressive society, a theme to which he returned in *Les Quatre Cents Coups* (1959, *The 400 Blows*), seemed to turn about face in *L'Enfant Sauvage* (1970, *The Wild Child*), a study of a wild child who grew up alone in the forest, based on an eighteenth-century case-history documented by Dr Itard. Although Truffaut, who himself plays Itard, was now apparently endorsing the values of society, the same insight into the true nature of children remained, a nature exaggerated by the unpromising resistance of the wild boy to

Child stars featured mainly in family entertainment, but films for children were on the increase

learning and the rules of society.

Other film-makers have seen the illogical, impenetrable world of childhood in more sinister fashion, as in the over-symbolic retreat into savagery of the marooned boys in *Lord of the Flies* (1963), the precocious evil masquerading as innocence in *The Bad Seed* or the children possessed by the devil in *The Exorcist* (1973) and *The Omen* (1976). But no film-maker has ever used childish anarchy with greater relish than Louis Malle in *Zazie dans le Métro* (1960, *Zazie*), a wild dash around Paris by a little girl who is equipped with a vocabulary of astonishing vulgarity and causes havoc wherever she goes.

During the Forties and Fifties, very few Hollywood films were made specifically with a child audience in mind; the box-office receipts were more to the point and if a recipe that mixed kids, animals and dollops of sentiment attracted the whole family, there seemed no reason to abandon it. *The Wizard of Oz* (1939) had proved a wonderful, magical delight; but the burden of children's entertainment fell largely to the animated fairy tales of Walt Disney and cartoon series such as Tom and Jerry and Bugs Bunny. Disney made his first incursion into live-action filming with *The Reluctant Dragon* (1941), in which Robert Benchley, playing a fictitious writer, visits the Disney studios. It was just a dramatized documentary but it gave Disney economic food for thought, since it had been far cheaper to produce than animation.

Live-action sequences were used in *The Three*

Above: Dean Stockwell with Gregory Peck as a crusading journalist in Elia Kazan's Gentleman's Agreement, *which attacked anti-Semitism. Top right: set at the time of the abortive 1905 uprising, Vladimir Legoshin's* Lone White Sail *was unrivalled at the time in the USSR for the acting of children (except by Mark Donskoy's* Gorky *trilogy). Below: Julie Andrews flies through the air in the magical* Mary Poppins

Caballeros (1945) and Disney became convinced that he could adapt to more conventional methods of film-making as well as persisting with his feature-length cartoons. He was persuaded by royalty money frozen in England during the war to make his first completely live-action film there. In Treasure Island, Long John Silver was played with melodramatic villainy reminiscent of an animated Disney baddie by Robert Newton, and the film's great success encouraged the new venture. Many more films were made with child-oriented themes – adventure, as in 20,000 Leagues Under the Sea (1954); animals, as in The Shaggy Dog (1959); family, as in Swiss Family Robinson (1960) – but they never measured up to the standards set by the animation features. It took some years before a real winner was found and a remarkable singing nanny, played by Julie Andrews, floated across the screen in Mary Poppins (1964).

There had been a tradition of film-making for children in both the Soviet Union and Japan since the Twenties, and the special facilities for production had resulted in at least one memorable Russian film, Legoshin's Lone White Sail (1938). The Eastern European countries make a special study of children's preferences and produce a wide range of

shorts and features for them; and since 1967 Indi has sponsored and distributed specialized feature through its government-aided Children's Fil Society.

Britain is unique in having an organizatio which has secured the cooperation of all sides of th film industry. Research commissioned by J. Arthu Rank in 1944 revealed what Disney could have tol him all along, that children prefer a simple stor with action rather than dialogue. The research, an the continued success of the rival Granad Children's Matinées, encouraged him to set up division within the Rank Organisation to mak films especially for children. This was succeeded i 1951 by the non-profit-making Children's Fil Foundation, which commissions and subsidize low-budget one-hour features for Saturda morning audiences. These features, technicall accomplished, aim to appeal to a child's intelligenc and need for adventure, and include some charm ing fantasies such as The Glitterball (1977). Neve theless the CFF's occasionally over-protective att tude has made the diet a little bland for TV-fed kid and falling audiences and the dwindling subsidy the film industry have put its future in doubt.

MARGARET FOR

EMI FILM PRODUCTIONS LTD. Presents

The Railway Children

Starring

DINAH SHERIDAN   JENNY AGUTTER   BERNARD CRIBBINS

With

WILLIAM MERVYN   SALLY THOMSETT   GARY WARREN

Based on the novel by E.Nesbit   Music by Johnny Douglas   Screenplay by Lionel Jeffries
Produced by Robert Lynn   Directed by Lionel Jeffries   TECHNICOLOR®
DISTRIBUTED BY ANGLO-EMI FILM DISTRIBUTORS LTD.

As the British film industry stumbled through the early Eighties, three films in particular – *Gregory's Girl, The Long Good Friday* (both 1980) and *Chariots of Fire* (1981) – testified to the immense talent among the ranks of British independent film-makers and to the fact that there were few immediate production outlets for the pictures they could have been making – and very little available cash.

The gangster thriller *The Long Good Friday*, directed by John MacKenzie originally for Associated Television, reached cinemas only after its producer, Barry Hanson, had fought to win for it a distribution deal with HandMade Films. Private finance, plus a distribution agreement with 20th Century-Fox, enabled the ace producer David Puttnam to make *Chariots Of Fire*, an exhilarating story of two athletes directed by Hugh Hudson, but in raising the money he had not ceased from mental fight for four years.

Bill Forsyth, a graduate of the National Film School whose only previous screen credits had been sponsored documentaries, first tried to sell the idea of *Gregory's Girl* to the British Film Institute (BFI) Production Board, but:

'The BFI managed to resist me and my script for two years running . . . . I would have jumped through flames for their £30,000, but it didn't come off . . . . The BFI didn't waste much ceremony in showing flops to the door.'

But even before this failure, Forsyth had begun working with the young performers at the Glasgow Youth Theatre on a regular basis. They represented the kind of movie-starved kids for and about whom he wanted to make films. With *Gregory's Girl* getting nowhere, he wrote and directed *That Sinking Feeling* (1979), a raw but pleasing comedy about a gang of unemployed Glasgow teenagers who make a night-time raid on a warehouse full of stainless-steel sinks, shot in 16mm and featuring members of the Youth Theatre. It was financed by an independent film-making collective, and its backers ranged from Shell and Marks & Spencer to the Strathclyde Regional Council, Wm. Brogan Grocers and Tennent Caledonian Breweries. This was film-making at a truly grass-roots level.

That Sinking Feeling was a hit at the 1979 Edinburgh Festival and later appeared at the London Film Festival. Though it did not go on general release, Forsyth now had that all-important first feature behind him and within three months had managed to get the producers Clive Parsons and Davina Belling to raise backing from Scottish Television and the National Film Finance Corporation for *Gregory's Girl*. So, through patience, persistence and initiative, Forsyth was able to realize his pet project.

Although *Gregory's Girl* was finally made for the modest budget of £210,000, it is hard to imagine how further expense could have improved it. Set in Cumbernauld New Town, near Glasgow, the film tells the story of Gregory, the gauche captain of a comprehensive school's football team, and his pursuit of the beautiful Dorothy, whose superior skills on the pitch have relegated him to goalkeeper. (Her selection is a popular choice – when she scores a goal, *both* teams rush to hug and kiss her.) From that unlikely premise, Forsyth constructs a delicious comedy, packed with laconic verbal and visual gags, that is short on dramatic action but unfolds from a patchwork of scenes of school life into a magical finish

Gregory's Girl

The beginnings of *Gregory's Girl* conjure up the image of the Scottish director Bill Forsyth setting out from Glasgow one morning, script in hand, somehow to beg, steal or borrow the necessary money from the film financiers in London. The years went by, the film was made, and London was charmed by an indigenously Scottish comedy hit that captures the daftest moments of everyone's youth with freshness, spontaneity and charming wit

Directed by Bill Forsyth, 1980
Prod co: Lake Film Productions/National Film Finance Corporation/Scottish Television. **prod:** Davin Belling, Clive Parsons. **sc:** Bill Forsyth. **photo** (colour): Michael Coulter. **ed:** John Gow. **art di** Adrienne Atkinson. **cost:** Nadia Arthur. **mus:** Colin Tully. **sd:** Louis Kramer. **football coach:** Donn McKinnon. **ass dir:** Ian Madden, Terry Dalzell. **r/t:** 91 minutes.
Cast: Gordon John Sinclair (*Gregory*), Dee Hepburn (*Dorothy*), Jake D'Arcy (*Phil Menzies*), Clar Grogan (*Susan*), Robert Buchanan (*Andy*), William Greenless (*Steve*), Alan Love (*Eric*), Carolin Guthrie (*Carol*), Carol Macartney (*Margo*), Douglas Sannachan (*Billy*), Allison Forster (*Madeline* Chic Murray (*headmaster*), Alex Norton (*Alec*), John Bett (*Alistair*), David Anderson (*Gregory's dad* Billy Feeley (*Mr Anderson*), Maeve Watt (*Miss Ford*), Muriel Romanes (*Miss Welch*), Patrick Lewsle (*Mr Hall*), Ronald Girvan (*Alan*), Pat Harkins (*Kelvin*), Tony Whitmore (*Gordon*), Denis Crima (*Richard*), Graham Thompson (*Charlie*), Natasha Gerson (*Brenda*), Christopher Higson (*penguin* members of the football teams of Our Lady's, Greenfaulds and Cumbernauld High Schools.

when Gregory finds himself in the midst of a summer-evening enchantment.

That notion of airy magic becomes fully apparent as Gregory falls victim to a female conspiracy. When Dorothy fails to turn up for their date, he goes for a walk with her messenger and is soon being passed from schoolgirl to schoolgirl as he traverses the town. Clearly there is something in the air, as one of his friends observes. Gregory finally ends up happily with Susan, who has fancied him all along. As a reward – and before kissing her goodnight after *she* has walked *him* home – he instructs her in 'horizontal dancing' (in which the dancers jive as they lie on the grass in the park), adding to the film's gallery of private and shared reveries. These include the delightful moments when Gregory, late for school, sidesteps an invisible opponent as he runs across the deserted playground; when the

headmaster is seen through an open doc playing to himself on the piano ('Off you go you small boys', he orders his astonishe spectators – who include the film audience when Menzies, the team coach, shows Doroth how to trap a football on her thigh in th changing room and the session turns into a improvised dance routine.

But *Gregory's Girl* is not just a world o dreamers. It is firmly rooted in reality, an Forsyth, once again extracting immaculat performances from his Youth Theatre cas proves that he is an especially acute observer o adolescent behaviour, particularly the contrasting ways boys and girls deal with eac other. The boys have no clue at all: Gregor thinks bulging biceps will win Dorothy; one o his friends, Andy, tries to impress two girls lunch with ridiculous facts; another, Stev prefers the problems of cookery; while Charli

op left: in the changing room, Gregory examines a fascinating bruise on Dorothy's knee after the football practice. Top: as Gregory and Charlie look on, Dorothy argues her claim to a place in the school football team with the coach Menzies. Top right: Susan rather likes Gregory, who has fallen for Dorothy; so Susan quietly bides her time

Above: Dorothy shows her skills on the football pitch and becomes the school's favourite pin-up. Below left: Dorothy, Margo and Carol plot how to get Gregory and Susan together. Below right: Gregory's sister Madeline discusses life and love with her own boyfriend. Right: production shot of the director Bill Forsyth on location for the film

evidently dumb. But their female classmates are ruthless and sophisticated. One brief shot shows Dorothy stifling a giggle at Gregory's attempts to ask her out. Looking down from a classroom window at the opposite sex cavorting in the playground, one girl describes to another the difference between boys and men in the short measure between her thumb and forefinger. Even Gregory's confidante, his 11-

year-old sister, Madeline, who has her own tiny boyfriend, is more wordly-wise than her big brother.

Is she Gregory's girl? Or is it Dorothy, or Susan? It hardly matters. Forsyth's hilarious and very real fable of love and football is in any case complete; it is a rare and challenging example of British film-making on the cheap and at its best.

GRAHAM FULLER

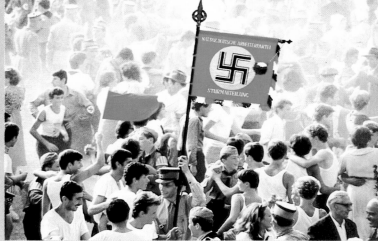

The Tin Drum is probably the best-known novel in post-war German literature and the one that elevated its author, Günter Grass, to international fame. But Grass's reputation was established in the Sixties when there was hardly any German cinema to speak of. As the 'New German Cinema' began to emerge in the Seventies, Grass received numerous offers to adapt The Tin Drum for the screen; however, it was not until he was approached by the director Volker Schlöndorff and the producer Anatole Dauman that he felt satisfied enough to accept.

Volker Schlöndorff had been involved from the start with the movement towards a new German cinema, and among his early films Der Junge Törless (1966, Young Törless) testified to his understanding of the pre-Nazi period of German history. Furthermore, his historical drama Der plötzliche Reichtum der armen Leute von Kombach (1971, The Sudden Fortune of the Poor People of Kombach) showed the kind of insight into a peasant community that was to stand him in good stead for The Tin Drum.

Grass himself collaborated on the adaptation of his novel for the screen, but many new ideas emanated from Jean-Claude Carrière, a regular screenwriter for the director Luis Buñuel, who brought his own surrealistic perspective to the story. The central theme of both novel and film is the decision of the boy Oskar not to grow up – his refusal to accept 'adult' society in all its bizarre behaviour. And Schlöndorff frequently offers the audience Oskar's viewpoint (for instance much of the film is shot from knee-level), thus translating the world of 'grown-ups' into a bizarre pantomine of sexual and political exploitation that sometimes reaches grotesque proportions. He succeeds in creating an image of the world which is peopled by grotesque marionettes with overblown ambitions and inflated desires. In the same way, the touring circus act which Oskar joins during World War II offers a commentary on wartime events that is all the more telling for being 'distorted' or parodied by dwarfs.

In this context, the style of the film emerges as more mythological

OSCAR AWARD
WINNER
BEST FOREIGN
LANGUAGE FILM

the Tin Drum

Produced by FRANZ SEITZ, VOLKER SCHLONDORFF and ANATOLE DAUMAN
Directed by VOLKER SCHLONDORFF Based on "THE TIN DRUM" by GUNTER GRASS
Screenplay by JEAN-CLAUDE CARRIERE, VOLKER SCHLONDORFF
and FRANZ SEITZ in collaboration with GUNTER GRASS
© 1979 Franz Seitz Film Bioskop Film Artemis Film Argos Films
(German Dialogue with English Subtitles)

than the easy blend of nostalgia and naturalism normally associated with films about this period. When Oskar disrupts a Nazi rally by beating his drum, the scene also functions on the level of fantasy. Similarly the compelling opening sequence in which the fugitive soldier hides beneath the woman's skirts conveys both the 'legend' of Oskar's parentage and the earthy realism appropriate to the location and period. Yet although The Tin Drum may look as if it is structured solely around a number of striking and potent images – most memorably the horse's head that is pulled out of the sea, crawling with live eels – it is nonetheless an impressively coherent narrative, especially considering the daunting task of adapting a book of just under six hundred pages.

As for the performances, there can be no doubt that David Bennent's portrayal of Oskar is unique. Schlöndorff knew that the part could not be played by a dwarf if audiences were to achieve the vital sense of empathy and hostility towards the character. Moreover Grass was insistent that Oskar should not be seen as a dwarf but simply as a child who had ceased to grow. A child actor was the only solution and when Schlöndorff discovered that the actor Heinz Bennent, (with whom he had worked before) had a son of 12 whose facial features were years in advance of the rest of his body, the casting problem was solved. Ironically the arrested development that David Bennent genuinely suffers from rendered it impossible for him to play Oskar as a mature adult in

post-war Germany and Schlöndorff had to abandon his original plan of following the novel right through to its conclusion.

Apparently very satisfied with the film's successful transition from book to screen, Günter Grass has gone on to enjoy a revival in popularity, assisted by the fact that the film won the Best Foreign Film Oscar for 1979. The re-creation of Grass's native city of Danzig (now Gdansk) is a fine testament to Igor Luther's photography (making effective use of strong autumnal light in his exteriors) and to the art direction of Bernd Lepel. Visually the film is breathtaking and the occasional appearance of present-day features in the landscapes only serves to underline the contemporary relevance of the film's message.   MARTYN AUTY

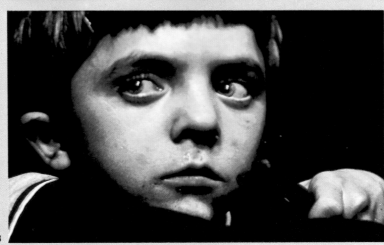

Directed by Volker Schlöndorff, 1979.
Prod co: Franz Seitz Film/Bioskop-Film/GGB 14 KG/Hallelujah-Film/Artemis Film/Argos Film/in association with Jadran Film and Film Polski. **exec prod:** Anatole Dauman. **prod:** Franz Seitz. **sc:** Jean-Claude Carrière, Franz Seitz, Volker Schlöndorff, from the novel by Günter Grass. **photo** (Eastman Colour): Igor Luther. **ed:** Suzanne Baron. **prod des:** Nicos Perakis. **art dir:** Bernd Lepel. **mus:** Maurice Jarre. **ass dir:** Branco Lustig. Alexander von Richthofen, Wolfgang Kroke, Andrzej Reiter, Richard Malbequi. **r/t:** 142 minutes. German title: *Die Blechtrommel*. Released in USA and GB as *The Tin Drum*.
Cast: David Bennent (*Oskar*), Mario Adorf (*Alfred Matzerath*), Angela Winkler (*Agnes Matzerath*), Daniel Olbrychski (*Jan Bronski*), Katharina Thalbach (*Maria Matzerath*), Heinz Bennent (*Greff*), Andréa Ferreol (*Lina Greff*), Fritz Hakl (*Bebra*), Mariella Oliveri (*Roswitha Raguna*), Tina Engel (*Anna Koljaiczek as a young woman*), Berta Drews (*Anna Koljaiczek as an old woman*), Roland Teubner (*Joseph Koljaiczek*), Tadeusz Kunikowski (*Uncle Vinzenz*), Ernst Jacobi (*Gauleiter Lobsack*), Werner Rehm (*Scheffler, the baker*), Ilse Pagé (*Gretchen Scheffler*), Kate Jaenicke (*Mather Truczinski*), Helmuth Brasch (*Heilandt*), Wigand Witting (*Herbert Truczinski*).

At the turn of the century in Poland, a peasant shelters a fugitive beneath her skirts and later gives birth to Agnes. After World War I, Agnes marries a Danzig grocer, Alfred Matzerath, but maintains her affair with her cousin Jan who may be the father of her son, Oskar.

At the age of three, Oskar resolves to stop growing. He becomes very attached to his toy drum (1), letting out a high-pitched scream capable of shattering glass if anyone tries to remove it.

In the city of Danzig, political upheaval is followed by the rise of the Fascist brownshirts (2). At a family outing (3) Alfred buys some eels that have been caught using a dead horse's head for bait, and later forces Agnes to eat them.

Agnes, pregnant by Alfred or Jan, loses the will to live and dies shortly afterwards. Oskar crawls for comfort beneath his grandmother's skirts (4). Alfred takes a young girl, Maria, to be his housekeeper and mistress, and then marries her (5).

Oskar leads Jan into the Polish post office which is under fire from the Germans (6). Jan is captured and executed. Through his friendship with a midget somnambulist, Roswitha (7), Oskar joins a circus which tours Europe performing for the Nazi top brass.

After the liberation, Oskar returns to Danzig where Alfred is shot as a collaborator. He resolves (8) to start growing again.

Joan Crawford once said: 'Of all the actresses, to me, only Faye Dunaway has the talent and class and the courage it takes to make a real star.' And it is Faye Dunaway who takes on the unenviable task of playing Joan Crawford in the film, *Mommie Dearest* (1981).

In many ways, the opening sequence says it all. Carefully avoiding a front view, the camera follows the morning routine of a busy, purposeful career woman who scrubs her face meticulously clean before plunging it into handfuls of ice, and signs photographs for fans while being chauffeured to the studio. Even from the back, Dunaway has clearly captured the essential Crawford characteristics and gestures – a certain kind of walk, a way of hunching the shoulders – so that when she finally turns to face the camera, it is no surprise that the resemblance is as strong as it is.

Crawford rose to stardom in the Thirties with such MGM movies as *Grand Hotel* (1932) and *Dancing Lady* (1933). Having started work as a shop-girl before moving to Broadway and then Hollywood, she often played characters from similar backgrounds: women of humble origins who as they become successful in business become losers in life. After leaving MGM in 1943, she had – with the exception of *Mildred Pierce* (1945), for which she won an Oscar – nothing but mediocre roles, only returning to form years later as the victimized crippled sister in *What Ever Happened to Baby Jane?* (1962). The popular image of Crawford is one of a star who was as unlucky in the films chosen for her as she was with the men she chose, but who nevertheless stamped her indelible personality and characteristics on all her roles.

Then, after she died in 1977, a new image emerged. Christine, her adopted daughter, published an autobiography, *Mommie Dearest*, which painted a picture of the much-loved star that was totally at odds with the legend of Joan Crawford. Crawford, as she appears in the book, is a domineering woman, obsessed with perfection and order in her home, her personal life, and, above all, in her children. The vision of Crawford elegantly attired in high heels and furs was replaced by one of her on her knees furiously scrubbing the bits of the living-room floor under the plant tubs which the maid had omitted to clean.

Transferring this melodramatic story of a tormented mother-and-child relationship from book to screen posed many difficulties, not the least of which was finding an actress who not only looked like Crawford, but who could at the same time convey both the public legend and the private neurosis in a sympathetic way. Dunaway rises to the occasion. Against a background of a luxurious, palatial Hollywood home, wearing glamorous dresses designed by the renowned costumier Irene Sharaff, Dunaway gives a superb performance which captures the magic of Crawford as well as conveying reasons for her destructive drive for perfection.

As Crawford's career begins to falter and her romantic attachments (combined for the film into one composite man) break up, her relations with her daughter deteriorate into a life-long battle of wills. Early fights in which Christina is faced with the same inedible plate of rare steak, meal after meal, until she gives in and eats it or the meat will rot where it stands, slowly give way to bursts of uncontrollable fury during which Crawford physically attacks her bewildered daughter. Yet through all the tantrums and bullying, Crawford indicates a desire to love and be loved; only that desire expresses itself in the determination to mould Christina into the ideal child. It is a desire that finally destroys any chance of the love she craves.

Dunaway has often played a kind of up-dated *femme fatale* in her films: *Bonnie and Clyde* (1967), *Chinatown* (1974) and *The Eyes of Laura Mars* (1978) all have echoes of that classic female of *film noir* whose allure destroys her lover by tempting him into crime. Crawford, as she is portrayed in *Mommie Dearest*, is a similar kind of woman, ruining the life of the daughter she longed for. It is Dunaway's forte and she brings to the part the credibility it needed.

At the end of the film, when Christina and her brother are cut out of their mother's will, Christina does not want to let Crawford have the last word – and she succeeds: *Mommie Dearest* will remain the screen image of Joan Crawford, a glamorous and legendary star in public and a frenzied, neurotic mother in private. SALLY HIBBIN

Directed by Frank Perry, 1981
Prod co: Paramount. **exec prod:** David Koontz, Terence O'Neill. **prod:** Frank Yablans. **assoc prod:** Neil A. Machlis. **sc:** Frank Yablans, Frank Perry, Tracy Hotchner, Robert Getchell, from the book by Christina Crawford. **photo** (Metrocolor, Panavision): Paul Lohmann. **sp eff:** Joseph P. Mercurio. **ed:** Peter E. Berger. **prod des:** Bill Malley. **art dir:** Harold Michelson. **cost:** Irene Sharaff. **makeup:** Charles H. Schram, Lee C. Harman. **mus:** Henry Mancini. **ass dir:** Michael Daves. **r/t:** 120 minutes.
Cast: Faye Dunaway (*Joan Crawford*), Diana Scarwid (*Christina Crawford*), Steve Forrest (*Greg Savitt*), Howard Da Silva (*Louis B. Mayer*), Mara Hobel (*Christina Crawford as a child*), Rutanya Alda (*Carol Ann*), Harry Goz (*Al Steele*), Michael Edwards (*Ted Gelber*), Jocelyn Brando (*Barbara Bennett*), Priscilla Pointer (*Mrs Chadwick*), Joe Abdullah (*captain*), Gary Allen (*Jimmy*), Selma Archerd (*Connie*), Adrian Aron (*woman guest*), Xander Berkeley (*Christopher Crawford*), Matthew Campion (*Bruce*), Carolyn Coates (*Mother Superior*), Jerry Douglas (*interviewer*), Margaret Fairchild (*Mother Superior at the orphanage*), Ellen Feldman (*Ginny*).

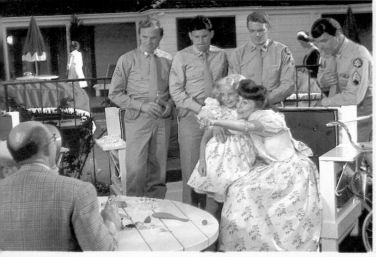

Joan Crawford (1), MGM's top film star, desperately wants a child. With her lover, Greg Savitt, she arranges to adopt first Christina (2), then Christopher. Joan is obsessed with perfection and discipline in her home and in her children. She insists, for instance, that their lavish Christmas presents, opened before the cameras of the press, should all be donated to a children's home.

With her career at MGM failing, Joan takes out her anger on her daughter in fits of temper (3). In rapid succession she is abandoned by Greg and is fired by Louis B. Mayer of MGM (4). She returns home and furiously destroys her rose bushes in the middle of the night (5).

After winning an Oscar for Best Actress in *Mildred Pierce*, her career revives but her emotional tantrums continue. Christina is sent to a private school where she is happy, but Joan removes her from it for a minor indiscretion (6), and sends her to a strict convent.

Joan marries Al Steele, chairman of the board of Pepsi Cola, and mother and daughter have a peaceful relationship for some years. When Steele dies, Joan starts drinking heavily and the battles begin again.

Nearing the end of her days, Joan is given a special award and Christina willingly accepts it for her (7) – publicly announcing that she loves her 'mommie dearest'.

Joan dies. Christina learns that she and her brother have been cut out of her mother's will (8). But Christina decides that Joan will not have the last word. . . .

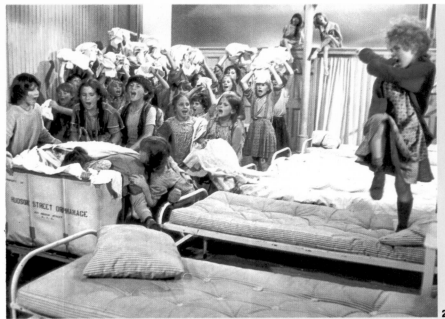

1

'Little Orphan Annie', a right-wing comic strip drawn by Harold Grey, was premiered in the *New York Daily News* in 1924, eventually reaching millions of people through syndication in over five hundred newspapers. In a 1937 survey the cartoon, with its little red-headed heroine, was declared the most popular comic strip in America.

Given the parallels between the economic climate of the Eighties and the period represented in the strip, there is a temptation to translate the main political message of the film *Annie* as meaning 'Let 'em eat cake' – the essential thrust, after all, of many a Thirties Depression musical, when opulent splendour was largely what the impecunious audience was paying to see. (In the Broadway show, this aspect of *Annie* was reportedly even broader.)

An attempt to liberalize the original strip to fit in with the Eighties seems to be behind a central sequence in the film in which Daddy Warbucks takes Annie and Grace to Washington DC to meet Franklin D. Roosevelt and his wife Eleanor;

they try (with the help of Annie singing 'Tomorrow') to persuade Warbucks to run one of the 'New Deal' youth employment programmes. Paradoxically, this scene and an earlier one – in which Warbucks leads a trip to the Radio City Music Hall to see the Rockettes and *Camille* (1936) – are the two which are the most accessible despite (or maybe because of) their profusion of period detail.

When Annie socks a couple of Lower East Side toughs, the graphic sound of her punches makes the cartoon-like stylization of the violence almost as pronounced as that of the bar-room brawls in Robert Altman's *Popeye* (1981). But unlike that film's revisionist approach to animated myth, which depends on collective memory and the passage of time, *Annie* has little room for psychological nuance (apart from the mugging of Carol Burnett's rather touchingly vulnerable villainess) and seeks instead to make the characters as easy to read and as unambiguous as the original button-eyed drawings of Harold Grey.   JONATHAN ROSENBAUM

5

Directed by John Huston, 1982
Prod co: Rastar Films Inc. **exec prod:** Joe Layton. **prod:** Ray Stark. **assoc prod:** Carol Sobieski. **sc:** Carol Sobieski. **photo** (Technicolor): Richard Moore **ed:** Michael A. Stevenson. **sup ed:** Margaret Booth. **prod des:** Dale Hennesey. **cost:** Theoni V. Aldredge. **mus:** Charles Strouse. **mus arr:** Ralph Burns. **lyrics:** Martin Charnin. **choreo:** Arlene Phillips. **prod exec:** Howard Pine.
Cast: Albert Finney (*Daddy Warbucks*), Carol Burnett (*Miss Hannigan*), Bernadette Peters (*Lily*), Ann Reinking (*Grace Farrell*), Tim Curry (*Rooster*), Geoffrey Holder (*Punjab*), Edward Herman (*Franklin D. Roosevelt*), Sandy (*himself*), Aileen Quinn (*Annie*), Roger Minami (*Asp*), Toni Ann Gisondi, Rosanne Sorrentino, Lara Berk, April Lerman, Robin Ignico, Lucie Stewart (*orphans*), Loni Ackerman, Murphy Cross, Nancy Sinclair (*the Boylan sisters*), I. M. Hobson (*Drake*), Lu Leonard (*Mrs Pugh*).

6

The Great Depression. Ten-year-old Annie escapes from a Manhattan orphanage (1) where she has been left with only half a locket and a note from her parents promising to return with the other half. Before she is found by the police and taken back to Miss Hannigan (2), the alcoholic tyrant who runs the orphanage, Annie saves a stray dog from the dog-catcher and names him Sandy; she also manages to sneak him back into the

orphanage with her.

Grace, personal secretary to billionaire Oliver Warbucks (3), turns up at the orphanage looking for a child to spend a week with her boss in order to help his public image. Annie charms herself and Sandy into the job (4), even though Warbucks had expected a boy, and after she and Sandy help Warbuck's bodyguards capture a bomb-throwing Bolshevik, he warms to her (5).

Grace, who finds herself deeply attracted to Warbucks, persuades him to adopt Annie, but after the signing of the adoption papers Annie expresses a desire to find her real parents. Warbucks offers a $50,000 reward on the radio, an action that inspires Miss Hannigan's jailbird brother Rooster and his girlfriend Lily to pose as Annie's parents (6). Miss Hannigan tells them she has the other half of the missing locket in her possession as it was sent to

her after Annie's parents' death. The other orphans get wind of the plot and go to Warbuck's house (7) to warn him, but Annie and the $50,000 cheque have already gone.

Warbucks sends the FBI and a private helicopter to rescue her (8) from death at the hands of Rooster, who plans to throw her off an old railroad drawbridge. At an enormous 4th of July party Grace and Warbuck's love is revealed (9), and they celebrate their reunion with Annie (10).

92

4

Annie

8

10

Index

Acknowledgments

Many of the illustrations come from stills issued to publicize films made or distributed by the following companies:
Action/FR3/Citel/Janus, Allied Artists, American International Pictures, Associated British Pictures, Boyd's Co, British Lion, Films du Carrosse/Sedif, Charles Chaplin Corporation, Childrens Film Foundation, Columbia, Daiei, © Walt Disney Productions, EMI, First National, Samuel Goldwyn, Hungarofilm, ITC/Lake Films/National Film Finance Corporation/Scottish Television,

Stanley Jaffe, MGM, Memorial, Films Montsouris/Films de France, Mosfilm, Paramount, Pickford Corporation, Film Polski, RKO, Rank, Rastar, Satjajit Ray Productions, Renown, Hal Roach, Saticoy, Franz Seitz Film/Bioskopfilm/Artemis Film/Hallelujah-Film/GGB 14KG/Argos Films/Paris Productions/Jadran/Film Polski, David O. Selznick, Seven Arts, Robert Stigwood, Film Produktion Arne Sucksdorff, Titanus, 20th Century Fox, Ufa, Ultramar Films, United Artists, Universal, Vanguard

Productions, Brent Walker, Hal B. Wallis, Warner Brothers, Wheel Films, The Who Films, Albert Zugsmith.

Although every effort is being made to trace the present copyright holders, we apologize in advance for any unintentional omission or neglect and will be pleased to insert the appropriate acknowledgment to companies or individuals in any subsequent edition of this publication.

Acknowledgments: Lindsay Anderson, Martyn Auty, Childrens Film Foundation, Harley Cockliss, Československý Filmový Ústav-Filmový Archiv, Walt Disney Productions, Greg Edwards Archive, Joel Finler Collection, Ronald Grant Archive, Archivio IGDA, ITC, Derek Jarman, Kobal Collection, Memory Shop New York, National Film Archive, David Robinson Collection, Steve Roe, Svenska Film Institut, Bob Willoughby.